On the Other Side of the Fence

From Dresden to America
A Memoir

Gisela Bierling-Greitzer

Xulon
PRESS

On The Other Side Of The Fence
From Dresden to America
by Gisela Bierling-Greitzer

Printed in the United States of America

ISBN 9781613790083

Unless otherwise indicated, Bible quotations are taken from
The King James Version (KJV) of the Bible. Copyright
© 1999 by American Bible Society; and The Holy Bible,
New International Version (NIV). Copyright © 1996 by
Broadman & Holman Publishers.

www.xulonpress.com

To our four children: Denise, Stephen, Kenneth, Frank
and to our fourteen grandchildren:
(Gisela) Lauren, Victoria, Jordann, Brandon,
Joseph, Daniel,
(Sabine) Matthew, Marissa, Brianna, Kyle, Connor,
Evan, Lukas, Asher

Stay proud and live righteously.

Foreword

M any of us are still filled with warmth and delight as we remember watching TV reruns preserved on CDs, DVDs, or VHS tapes. The rapid pace of life today and the evolution of invention and new technologies make the eight-track tape, prehistoric; the cassette tape, nostalgic; the VHS tape, old. There is but one method that remains timeless to preserve our thoughts and memories—the written word.

Man from the earliest of days has sought to record history and the events of daily life for various specific reasons. Modern technology has allowed us to preserve with archival precision stories of families, a life gone by, to the struggles of families during the various wars of the twentieth century and their early years of settling in America.

Although this book was originally intended for the author's children and grandchildren, it is nevertheless an insightful and touching account to any reader, as this is a story not covered by ordinary school curriculum or news media.

The reader will follow one particular family from its life in Germany in the early 1900s, through the desperation of World War II, and finally to emigration to the United States. Personal recollection of the author and stories told by family members, surprisingly well-preserved ancestral documents, and the use of the Internet became immeasurable tools for the accuracy of the accounts described in this book. It is no doubt a story of courage and adventure, determination and drive, sacrifice and suffering, gratitude, personal discipline, and trust, all built upon a solid foundation of love of life and family. Each word, line, paragraph, and page radiates a beauty and love not frequently found in books today.

The title *On the Other Side of the Fence* becomes clear and obvious as the reader follows the exciting journey of the Bierling family through years of both hardship and joy. The reader will realize that as we go through life, there will always be another side that presents itself, whether it deals with the opposing sides of conflict or war, nationality, politics, religion, rules and regulations, or personal views and opinions. The list is endless.

While this is a personal story of a family's journey to America, it contains a significant amount of objective historical data that was a real part of this family's everyday life. The author is not a historian but the fact she lived through these events of history and lived to document the details for her children and grandchildren gives this story a solid place in the written accounts of that period of time. This story is a special gift she leaves to her family and with humility allows us, the reader, to partake in it.

The historical facts contained within this story have been and will continue to be analyzed and documented by various historians. We must, however, not forget that what happened to this family and many other innocent families during this period was real and associated with an immense amount of personal and communal suffering. The author seeks not to condemn or to dramatize these facts of history. She does, however, want those reading this story to see the truth behind the events she described. In other words, the citations (foot & endnotes) contained within this book should prompt anyone to want to further their knowledge of the objective data of historical occurrences. It clearly represents a significant part of who the Bierling family is and how living through these episodes of the past defined them as persons and immigrants to this great country we call the United States of America.

The reader will learn about the life of the author and her family, as well as the history of a culture, people, and nation. The story presents the interesting viewpoint of a family who has been on the other side of the fence.

George F. Zerucha *
M.T.S., PA-C

* George F. Zerucha, M.T.S, PA-C is the nephew and godson of the author. He holds a Masters degree in Sacred Pastoral Theology. He has practiced for 20 years as a Board certified (PA-C) Physician Assistant in Emergency medicine & Family Practice and spent most of his career in rural America in medically underserved areas. He is fluent in the German language and provided patient care in Portuguese, Spanish and German.

Contents

꧁꧂

1

Our Family Tree

My father, Alfred Bierling, very diligently made sure that our family tree was preserved and kept up-to-date. He did so by making handwritten updates in our family tree hardcover book. This family tree, originally written and distributed by Heinrich Oscar Bierling in 1919, actually begins with our forefather Hans Bierling (1584–1640). Research into earlier descendents was unattainable, as the family's records had been destroyed in two separate church fires in Gera, Germany, during the sixteenth and seventeenth centuries. Furthermore, previous family registries had been destroyed during the devastating epoch of the Thirty Year War.

We came upon all those records and documents after both our parents had passed away and we soon realized what a rare, valuable treasure our father secured for us, his descendents. As you read my story, you may wonder (as did I) how was it possible to recover all that documented information? The only explanation I have is that my father's older siblings, Robert and Luise, were most likely the ones who were instrumental in supplying a great deal of the background to him. He then embarked on his own mission to further research and uncover all there is to know about our family and diligently made the necessary entries in our family tree book. Not an easy task to accomplish without the use of the Internet, the electronically advanced source of information of nowadays!

My father collected and filed all available personal documents, such as birth, marriage, and death certificates, and put together a photo album that depicted all the pertinent family members (whom he called the "old-timers") as the link to our ancestry and heritage within the Bierling family

I had many conversations with my father as we sat on his porch in Crestwood Village, Whiting, New Jersey. It was always such a treat to spend this precious time with him. While sharing a glass of Beaujolais, his favorite wine, I listened to him talk about his youth as the fourth of five children of Friedrich Robert Max Bierling and his wife Elsa. I eagerly absorbed his nostalgic account about the great house located on Wienerstrasse in Dresden, which our grandfather built.

My father described the layout of this house so precisely that I could envision it clearly in my mind. Upon entering the mansion, you noticed an imposing staircase to the right leading to the upper floors where my grandparents' bedroom, the bedrooms for the children, and the bathroom were located. Since there were five children in the family, all rooms were well occupied. An indoor balcony encircled the entire upper floor.

The main floor on the ground was occupied by the living room, dining room, library, and billiard room. The chauffeur, the butler, and the cook lived in the level below the main floor, which had a separate entrance for the service staff and deliveries. The kitchen and laundry room were located there as well. The maids who attended to the family lived in the upper floor near the roof. If I recall correctly, my father mentioned that the house was equipped with dumbwaiters to facilitate access to the roof for hanging the laundry to dry, as well as transporting food dishes to and from the dining areas.

It was quite a setup for those days, but perfectly suitable for a wealthy and renowned family such as the Bierlings. Today the room to the immediate left on the main floor displays an oil painting still left from the Bierling era.

May I now present the tenth generation of the Bierling family who were brought up in that house, all offsprings of

Paternal Grandparents
*Friedrich Robert Max (1867–1936) and Elsa Bierling
(1873–1923)*

Luise Bierling	Born 1/30/1894	Unmarried
Gertraud Bierling	Born 4/18/1895	Unmarried
Robert Bierling	Born 4/16/1896	Died 4/17/1896
Robert Bierling	Born 11/11/1898	Married – one son

Robert Max	*Born 5/10/1926*	*Died 9/06/1945 while clearing land mines*
Alfred Bierling	Born 6/16/1903	Four children
	Michael, Gisela, Thomas, Sabine	
Heinz Bierling	Born 7/13/1908	Died at Russian front, 1945
	One son, *Rolf*	*(no other data available)*

When my brother Tom and I visited this once beautiful city in June of 1994, four years after the reunification of the two Germanys, it was as if an invisible hand led us to the street and the house of our forefathers. We had never been in Dresden, nor did we have any idea how to find Wienerstrasse. We only knew that it was near the *Hauptbahnhof* (main railroad station). Tom and I had met at Berlin Tempelhof Airport, then rented a car and headed south to find both Dresden, the birthplace of our father (tenth generation), as well as the nearby town of Pulsnitz, the birthplace of the four eleventh generation Bierling offsprings: Michael (Micha or Mike), Gisela (Gila), Thomas (Tom), and Sabine (Bine). Actually, I must correct this statement: Mike, our oldest sibling, was born in Dresden; the rest of us were born in Pulsnitz.

As Tom and I approached Dresden in 1994, we encountered traffic congestion during afternoon rush hour and decided to take side streets at random to escape this impossible situation. We chose a street, just any street, and later discovered that according to the city map, we were heading directly into the part of town where we needed to be. Were we just lucky, or was it fate? GPS was unheard of in those days.

After a few left turns and right turns as we were trying to find our way, we came upon the main railroad station (Hauptbahnhof) and by sheer coincidence also our hotel, which we had selected by pointing a finger on a hotel listing while we were still in New York. The hotel was located directly across the street from the Hauptbahnhof on Prager Strasse. We checked our map again and discovered that Wienerstrasse actually intersected with Prager Strasse right at the Hauptbahnhof.

It was only a few blocks away, so we easily reached Wienerstrasse and soon found the great old mansion. In actuality, we were drawn to one particular house that resembled a painting we had seen on a wall in our parents' home. We looked at each other and simply nodded, yes this was the house. It seemed to beckon us as if it knew us and welcomed us to come closer. We just stood there in total awe and felt as if we had been transported into another time—that of my father's childhood. Without looking for the house number, we just knew we had found the old Bierling residence that had ended around the beginning of World War II when the family was scattered and later many members perished.

Since our trip to Dresden took place only a short time after the reunification of the two Germanys (East and West), Tom and I were still a bit nervous about traveling as Westerners in former East Germany. Deep-rooted refugee complex, I suppose. In addition, in the backs of our minds were the disturbing reports and condemning reputation of the East German government relayed to us by friends and family members who had been trapped in that part of Germany under the Communist regime throughout the years since 1945. Unsure of ourselves, we did not have the nerve to ring a bell to talk to one of the inhabitants to get updated information on the house.

We did walk to the back of the house, though, to see the "glorious rose garden," as my father had described it, which my grandfather had so diligently and lovingly nurtured. We envisioned it according to our father's description, but as it turned out, and not quite unexpectedly, we were faced with disappointment. The garden was very small, probably reduced to less than half, as we noticed parking garages where the rest of the garden had been. I suppose this space in the center of Dresden had become valuable and precious over the four years since the reunification.

Life in this big city had taken on a renewed character and productivity since that momentous reunion with the West, much like a sleeping giant awaking after a forty-five-year dormant state and briefly stretching its limbs before getting to work to make up for lost time. Advanced technology and productivity, influenced by the West, had also brought to market a greater number of automobiles, and thus parking spaces pushed their way into the city landscape.

Sabine, the youngest of the eleventh generation of the Bierling family, traveled to Dresden with her husband a few years later, and they too were drawn directly to the family mansion on Wienerstrasse. She did have a chance to speak with a resident whom she met outside the gate and who, although initially rather defensive and suspicious of Westerners, provided many details about its postwar history. Once my sister mentioned the name *Bierling* and our relation to that name, the woman became more willing to share her information. She knew all about our grandfather, the entrepreneur and investor in the city of Dresden, as well as the history of the mansion. Feeling more comfortable, she then invited my sister and her husband to enter.

Sabine described her experience when they came upon this foreboding homestead and then stepped into the great entry hall as something out of *The Twilight Zone*. The halls, the large staircase, and the doors to the various rooms, plus an old painting of Dresden still hanging in one of the rooms downstairs created visions of the past, the old Bierling days. It touched her very deeply. Being present on location gave her a sense of coming home, although she had never been there before.

Although the great house was apparently sold in 1936 to a corporation, some time after the War this mansion was turned over by repossession from private ownership to the People of Dresden. The city then appointed a caretaker for the old Bierling residence, who subsequently divided and assigned the house to individual tenants. Today the great house on Wienerstrasse still maintains apartments as well as a small business operation.

We will always uphold the memory of our forefathers, the Bierlings, who had loved Dresden and were so much a part of it. Some day in the near future, Sabine, Tom, and I plan to revisit this great city, sadly without our brother Mike, who passed away in September 2006.

At this point, it is timely to explain the recognition of the Bierling name in Dresden and the dedication and love all the Bierlings held for this city as far back as the 1800s. It is unmistakably evident that the Bierling family left a mark on this great city.

For instance, Albert Christoph Bierling (8th generation), born November 21, 1824, founder of the Dresden Art and Bell Foundry, cast many exquisite bronze monuments, such as the statue of King Johann (on horse) of 1889, which is located in the theater plaza in front of Semper Opera, as well as the Bismarck memorial cast in 1903. Between 1883 and 1913 his foundry produced over five hundred church belfries and over two thousand bronze bells, some can still be heard throughout Germany and various lands. His firm, the C. Albert Bierling Company in Dresden was later continued by his two sons (9th generation), Albert Clemens Bierling (born August 23, 1852) and Albert Bruno Bierling (born January 6, 1854) until 1922 when their operation ended. [1]

One of the bronze statues, the Martin Luther Memorial (1885), cast by Albert Christoph Bierling according to the sculpture by Adolf von Donndorf, is located in front of Dresden's Frauenkirche. The head was cast from a plaster model by Ernst Rietschel originally designed for the Luther memorial statue in the city of Worms. Interestingly, Ernst Rietschel was born in Pulsnitz, our birth place. An article found in the 2005 German *Life* magazine, written by Ben Henkey, describes the horrible bombing of Dresden in 1945. The article is illustrated with a picture of the Martin Luther statue lying strewn amidst the rubble in front of the fraction of remains of the Frauenkirche following the World War II bombing.

His foundry's twin fountains Still Waters and Stormy Waves are considered to be the most beautiful fountains in Dresden, and so is a group figure at the Dresden town hall called Children with Dog, which was donated by Councillor of Commerce, Oskar Bierling.

It is also fitting to note that on November 8, 1889, among the three financiers of the newly founded horse-drawn streetcar company in Dresden was our grandfather, Hermann Robert Bierling (9th generation), the owner and director of a well-known leather manufacturing plant. I understand that at one point in time he opted to sell his leather processing plant rather than move it to the outskirts of Dresden, as it was urgently suggested. Thus he yielded to ongoing neighborhood complaints about the unpleasant odor that was emitted by the leather treatment solutions during processing.

The new streetcar company launched its first horse-drawn line between Friedrichstrasse and the Fuerstenstrasse. In 1891, two depots were purchased, which held up to thirty tram cars each. The population of Dresden was growing, and ever-increasing industrialization created greater distances between home and workplace. This resulted in the public's request for cheap and well-run mass transportation. In 1892, the German Red Company tram line (even numbered) owned 399 horses and eighty tram cars. This was in direct competition with the English Yellow Company (odd numbered). Both shared the same tracks. In the year 1900, the streetcar network was being changed to an electric line. On December 30, 1905, the City of Dresden took over both competing private lines to consolidate the transportation network as one fleet, thus ensuring a uniform network.

Now back to the original financiers of the newly founded streetcar company. The other two contributors were the owner of the sawmill Grumbt, and engineer Oskar Schwab. All three founded and financed the German Streetcar Company in Dresden with a donation of six million marks, which was a lot of money in those days. Note here that the Grumbt family and the Bierlings, as well as the Decarlis, my mother's family, had been long-time friends.

The close friendship between these families continued throughout the years and was further nurtured between my mother and Irmgard Grumbt, a descendant of the Grumbt family in Dresden. Irmgard and our mother had known each other since childhood when they spent their summer vacations at a castle in Sluknov, Czechoslovakia, approximately 65 km east of Dresden. Irmi's grandfather had purchased this castle for the family's summer vacations and declared that the children in the family were allowed to invite a friend as often as they wished. At times this amounted to ten children altogether. Since our mother was Irmi's best friend, she was privileged to enjoy wonderful, unforgettable times there of which our mother often spoke with glee. These joyful visits at the castle continued into their young adulthood until they each set out to pursue their individual dreams, privately and professionally. The friendship that Irmi and our mother enjoyed never diminished but continued throughout the years, after each of their marriages, the arrival of their children, through World War II, my mother's emigration to America, and way beyond till the death of my mother at age seventy-six in 1986. Irmgard died twelve years later in 1998.

Tante Irmi, as we called her, had two children, with whom she lived in a small town near Munich. The friendship between the two mothers was later carried over to us, the eleventh generation Bierling siblings, who are now close with Tante Irmi's son, Joerg, and his wife, Gerda. To this day, whenever we visit Germany, either Joerg and Gerda's home or Munich itself is our designated meeting place. Sometimes we arrange to meet in Garmisch-Partenkirchen or Oberammergau at the foot of the Bavarian Alps to hike the mountain range and meadows, just as our mothers did so many times during all those years past.

Friends for life — Elsie and Irmi

Left to right, Joerg, Gisela, Sabine, Thomas, Gerda
Munich May 2009

2

Our Parents' Love Story

My father was born in Dresden on June 16, 1903, while my mother was born in Tsingtau, China, in 1910, where her father was the director of the Deutsche Bank. I believe it was in China where her father, Felix Schmidt Decarli, saw Ada Morrison riding in a rickshaw and decided on the spot that he would marry her. They married indeed. I am not sure of the date, but I found a notarized translation of my grandmother Ada's birth and baptism documents dated Hong Kong, September 21, 1904. I assume that these papers were required for their wedding.

Their first child, Alice, was born in Kobe, Japan, on November 26, 1906. Her sister, my mother Elsie, was born in Tsingtau, a German colony in China, on July 16, 1910.

My grandmother Ada Morrison was of British descent, born to John Morrison and Maria Mahon of Wales. Is this complicated enough for you? It certainly took a lot of research into our ancestry, and I am glad that I could open up at least a small window to our roots.

Maternal Grandparents
Felix Decarli *Ada Decarli nee Morrison*
1873–1933 *1884–1932*

When the German colony in China was dissolved in 1914 with the beginning of World War I, all German citizens had to return to their homeland. Thus my mother, her sister Alice, and her parents took the long journey by ship to Germany and settled again in Dresden. As the three families, the Bierlings, the Decarlis, and the Grumbts enjoyed a close relationship, so did their children.

Often the kids would play hide-and-seek in the big mansion on Wienerstrasse, and my father, seven years older than my mother, would scoop her up and hide her successfully so she wouldn't be "it" to end the game. Often he would carry her on top of his shoulders when it was too difficult for her to keep in step with the others. Many, many years later as adults, the brother of my mother's best friend, Irmi, quietly confessed that he had secretly harbored special feelings for my mother as early as the games in the Bierling mansion or the summer castle. But my father got to her first, and what a good match it was! The aforementioned kids eventually went through their schooling and higher education and then scattered to pursue their professional endeavors.

My mother followed her parents from Dresden to live in Cologne, where she completed her administrative schooling and began her working career. It was a difficult time for her, as her mother soon became incapacitated with a serious lung ailment that required my mother to take care of her as well as her father; she was in her early twenties. She lost both of them one year apart, her mother first and a year later her father, who died of a broken heart. My mother was devastated. I am not sure whether this was her reason for leaving Cologne and returning to Dresden, but it would have made sense.

As far as our father was concerned, after completing his education and practice in the field of commerce and trade, he took a position with Shell Oil in London. During his time in London, he lived with a Jewish family, the Rothchilds, who had taken in this charming young man from Germany and treated him very well. He remained in London for a number of years and then returned to Dresden.

One might ask what higher guidance or fate arranged for my parents to be on the same train when they had their surprise reunion as young adults. My mother described the scene often with a sentimental smile and recalled that she was traveling home from an away game with her field hockey team (athletics were her pastime passion). Since she was the goalie, she was all scraped up, dirty, tired and not at all in a good mood, since they had lost the game to boot. In plain language, she was miserable and somewhat cranky.

And who should come walking down the aisle of the train towards my mother? Yes, my handsome, dapper, and charming father, looking something like Clark Gable! My mother could have crawled into her duffle bag, she was so embarrassed. My father was somewhat amused when he saw my mother's obvious awkwardness but also extremely happy to recognize that he had just linked up with that shy little girl of so many years ago. Dirty or not, she was beautiful.

After my mother overcame her first urge to hide and realized who this handsome young man actually was, she immediately made an emotional connection with my father. This was the real beginning for them. They were married on February 7, 1935, at the Lutheran Christuskirche in Dresden. The marriage verse they chose was from Mark 11:22: "Have faith in God" (KJV). They lived in Dresden until they moved to Pulsnitz shortly after the birth of their first child, my brother Michael, who was born on July 16, 1936.

I invite you now to follow the rest of their journey through life by reading on. Before I continue with their story, though, I would like to credit my parents with the special and noble ways in which they conducted their lives, how they related to each other and the world around them. Their actions were without fail carried out with love and devotion, consideration and selflessness. Throughout their lives, this never changed and was quite obvious to people around them. They were indeed a remarkable couple, a wonderful example to others.

When they grew old and were living in a retirement community, they were widely known as the "newlyweds" among the other senior citizens because whenever they walked together—and they did a lot of that—they always held hands or linked arms. My father regularly brought her flowers and treated her with much kindness and respect; it was heartwarming—an occurrence so rare in our society today.

At age seventy-three, my father became very ill and needed urgent prostate surgery, delayed for a year because of his emphysema and the fear of respiratory problems developing during the surgery. At that time, my father already needed the assistance of a machine to regulate his breathing. My mother lovingly and devotedly cared for him until the day she needed to drive him to the hospital for the surgery. He was in extreme pain and could hardly walk, yet on the way there, he asked her to stop at the flower store. He insisted on taking those steps by himself while my mother waited in the car, still objecting. The walk was slow and the purchase took a long time, but he emerged holding a bouquet of carnations, which my mother loved so much, and brought them to her.

My father barely survived the surgery, went into respiratory arrest as feared, was shocked back to life, and lingered hopelessly and in despair in the hospital until he slipped into a coma and passed away. Tom and Sabine made the trip to the hospital in Toms River, New Jersey, (as did Mike and I) numerous times during the three weeks after the surgery. We took turns, but each time it was necessary to return to our respective families and jobs in our hometowns.

My brother Mike and I happened to be with my father when we realized he was taking a turn for the worse. It had been our turn to relieve our mother, who had been by his side the entire time. We immediately summoned our mother to return to the hospital and called Tom and Sabine once we realized the end was near. They came to his bedside as quickly as they could, Tom from Nassau County, New York, and Sabine from Bucks County, Pennsylvania. Unfortunately, all three arrived too late, only to find that he had slipped out of consciousness. We all took turns to quietly sit vigil by his bedside to the end, each involved in his or her own emotional torment.

The doctor had asked whether we wanted my father on a life support device, but we told him about our father's wish not to prolong his life when it came to that. You see, before the surgery, there had been a moment when the entire family was together on a typical Sunday when my father requested that we all gather around the table. My father cleared his throat, as he always did when he had something important to say, and we listened to his last wishes, which included his request not to be put on life support equipment. So when the time came, we complied and with aching hearts let him slip from his coma into death. When it was over, we all had the same thought, although tortured by our loss: *He is now at peace*. It had been a long struggle for him.

The trip home from the hospital was eerily quiet. My mother was clearly holding back her emotions, and we let her. Once we arrived at her home, where we would all spend the night, she slowly and without a word retreated to her (their) bedroom and gently closed the door. We could only imagine the pain she felt at losing her life partner. How sad. His carnations would wilt in time, but certainly not her or our memories of him.

At age fifteen, when my father was confirmed in the Lutheran Erloeserkirche of Dresden on April 13, 1919, he chose his life promise: "Be thou faithful unto death" (Revelation 2:10, KJV), and "Hold on to what you have, so that no one will take your crown" (Revelation 3:11, NIV).

Indeed, he lived his life accordingly, and no one ever took his crown!

So typical of my father, he had the loving foresight to make preparations in the event of his demise. He created a folder which included detailed instructions regarding life insurance policies, social security, pension and other sources of income and liabilities, relevant contact information for banks and authorities as well as important medical and personal updates. Once our mother stabilized her emotions, she was able to follow step-by-step on how she was to proceed to set up life without him. This was also the time when we located the updated family tree book mentioned earlier.

Our mother lived another nine years after he passed away, but it was obvious to us that she had lost her spirit and was very lonely, even though she had her children and an increasing number of grandchildren. Throughout the years that followed my father's death, she was extremely restless and often flew back to Germany. This was afforded through Lufthansa's gracious extension of my father's life benefits to our mother. Her many trips to Germany lead in particular to Garmisch-Partenkirchen, where our parents had enjoyed so many happy vacations together in the midst of the breathtaking Bavarian alpine landscape and its friendly country folks. On those occasions, she would always meet up with Irmi, Thea and Otto Grumbt (Irmi's brother), and my father's sister, Tante Lis, who, not always but often, joined the group after obtaining permission from the East German government to leave her home in Dresden to travel to the West. All were members of the old crew of childhood playmates at the Bierling mansion on Wienerstrasse.

My mother later moved away from the homestead in Crestwood Village, Whiting, New Jersey, to be closer to my sister, Sabine, in Pennsylvania. The decision to leave the home she had contentedly and peacefully shared with my father was in the end not at all the solution she was looking for. She felt like a fish out of water, although she was so close to my sister. Her emphysema became increasingly debilitating, and she too needed to rely on an oxygen tank to breathe. (Oh, those many years of smoking!) In addition, she had to deal with osteoporosis, which curved her back to such a point that it infringed on her breathing.

It occurs quite frequently that families have to watch hopelessly as one or the other parent becomes irreversibly enveloped in a 'fog' of memory loss or dementia later on in their lives even though their bodies are functioning relatively well. In my mother's case the reverse was reality. Her mind was as sharp as a tack but she became increasingly annoyed about the fact that her body was failing her. Osteoporosis and emphysema raked havoc on her fragile body.

On one of our visits to her home, she asked my husband and me whether we would drive her to my father's grave back in Crestwood Village. We gladly obliged and took her on the one-hour drive to the Keswick cemetery. She got out of the car and stood in front of the grave for a long time while we stayed back to grant her the privacy of the moment. Then she turned around and wordlessly reentered the car, and we drove home in silence. It seemed to us that she had told my father that she would be joining him soon. Indeed, it was the last time she was out of her home on her own free will.

Her decline was rather rapid. In and out of hospital stays, she moved for a short time to my sister's home, who had lovingly prepared her home to accommodate my mother's medical condition. But then she needed to be placed in a nursing home with around-the-clock professional attention.

My daughter and I visited her at the nursing home shortly before she passed away. We found her sitting in a chair next to her bed watching television and commenting on a championship tennis match she was watching attentively. We spent precious moments with her, combed her hair and gently rubbed lotion onto her dry arms and legs, although she initially waved it off as not being necessary. Before we left we helped her into bed and gently kissed her goodbye. We were on our way out of the nursing home when I had the inexplicable urge to turn around and go back to her room to look at her again, and there she sat appearing so small, like a bird, giving me that sweet smile that broke my heart then and still does as I remember that moment. Our mother died peacefully (thank God) in her sleep just two days later. She was laid to rest beside my father, and thus a true love story ended.

In memory, we hold our parents close to our hearts and realize over and over just how special they were, presenting themselves as good examples of righteousness and decency with uncompromising love and dedication to their family, friends, and neighbors.

3

Demise of a City

Now here's a recap of what happened to Dresden towards the end of World War II in February 1945. In the last year of the war, Dresden had become a hospital/Red Cross city. During those final months of World War II, Dresden became a safe haven to some 600,000 refugees, consisting mainly of women, children, and the elderly. The flood of refugees fleeing from the advancing Red Army from miles away arrived by overcrowded trainloads, on foot, or by horse-drawn wagons and by February 1945 swelled the city's population to over 1.2 million, doubling the number of inhabitants. Schools, hospitals as well as private homes within Dresden and surrounding towns housed as many as possible of the thousands of refugees streaming into town. All thought they would be safe there. Little did they know, however, that the city had been left defenseless and they were about to die.

Dresden was a center of cultural and architectural wonders, including the famous Zwinger Museum and Palace and the cathedral, the Frauenkirche (Church of Our Lady). There were no military objectives of any consequence in the city—its destruction could do nothing to weaken the Nazi war machine. U.S. and British air warfare had left Dresden intact until that point.

The Soviet military forces were poised to seize the city from the Nazis. It was at that moment that the military and political strategists of Britain and the United States decided to launch a terror bombing attack. [2]

An internal Royal Air Force memo in January 1945 described the plans as such: "Dresden, the seventh largest city in Germany and not much smaller than Manchester, is also by far the largest unbombed built-up area the enemy has got. In the midst of winter, with refugees pouring westwards and troops to be rested, roofs are at a premium. The intentions of the attack are to hit the enemy where he will feel it most, behind an already partially collapsed front, to prevent the use of the city in the way of further advance, and incidentally to show the Russians when they arrive what Bomber Command can do." [3]

Winston Churchill was Britain's prime minister then. He was also responsible for war strategy, especially regarding its political aims. Churchill's goal in Europe was not only to destroy the military machine of Britain's imperialist rival—Germany—but to stop the advance of the Soviet Union. With the latter in mind, he decided to bomb Dresden.

No one really quite understood the persistence on Churchill's part to inflict maximum destruction on Dresden's population. Quite possibly, in addition to the above mentioned reasoning, it may also have been an act of revenge for the blitz attacks by Germany on London from September 7, 1940, to May 10, 1941, and then again in 1944 with the use of V-1 and V-2 rockets terrorizing the London population and resulting in many casualties. Perhaps it was a typical tit-for-tat for which the innocent ordinary citizen—not the war machine—on either side suffered the consequences.[4] This is how war works: the victor writes history, and in most cases, it is recalled with a one-sided perspective—the winner's. But there are always two sides to a story.

The goal of the western Allies, Great Britain and the U.S., was not only to inflict maximum destruction and loss of life, but also to show their Communist "allies" what a capitalist war machine could do—sheer muscle flexing to leave an impression. It was clearly a political move rather than a military one. More realistically, though, it would also disrupt and confuse the German civilian population behind the lines and thus bring the German beast to its knees and speed up the end of the war in Europe. And so it did, just as the U.S. succeeded in Hiroshima later that same year—but at what cost of human lives in each case!

There was never any doubt on the part of the British Allies what and whom they would be bombing at Dresden. They knew exactly yet did not clarify their reasons or rationale to the British airmen who were called to execute the order to firebomb the city. The war was transferred from the military battlefield to the civilian population with the intent to eliminate all human beings on the ground. We were those people on the ground.

The attack on Dresden was among the last of a long string of city attacks throughout Germany that began in 1940. City by city, Germany was laid waste. The attack on Hamburg in July of 1943 left at least 40,000 dead civilians, among them 7,000 children and young adults. None of the large German cities were spared. Targeted and destroyed between 1940 and 1945 were German cities that carried significant strategic importance, whether they were harbors like Rotterdam, Bremen, and Hamburg; industrial centers like Cologne, Düsseldorf, Schweinfurt, Braunschweig, Stuttgart, and Nuremberg, to name just a few; or political seats, like Munich and of course Berlin, the capital of Germany at that time and the seat of Hitler and his echelon. Berlin alone endured seventeen air attacks by the Allies. Sir Arthur Harris suggested that the main attack on Berlin (Operation *Thunderclap*) should be supplemented by simultaneous operations of a like nature against Chemnitz,

Leipzig and Dresden which, equally to Berlin, would share the task of housing evacuees from the East... [5]

Why did I choose to discuss the fate of Dresden in particular, and why does the mention of Dresden leave a sense of uneasiness with so many? In February 1945, Germany was already crumbling and in disarray. The bombing of Dresden was unnecessary and remains one of the more controversial Allied actions of the western European theatre of war. (I really don't like the expression "theatre of war" as often depicted by historians). Later, after the horrific results of this attack became known, Churchill tried to distance himself from this action in a memo dated March 28, 1945, that was sent to Air Marshall Arthur Harris and General Ismay for the British chiefs of staff and the chief of the air staff. [6]

In its prime, in the prewar days, Dresden was known for its delicate Meissen china and its baroque and rococo architecture. Because of its overall beauty, it was called "Florence on the Elbe." It was the center of Europe's cultural scene, with renowned theaters, a grand opera house (Semper Opera), and countless museums. Its galleries housed works by Vermeer, Rembrandt, Rubens, and Botticelli. On the evening of February 13, none of this would matter.

And then came the fateful moment when the city of Dresden was systematically bombed on February 13, 14, and 15, as ordered by Winston Churchill of Great Britain and executed by Sir Arthur "Bomber" Harris, the British chief air marshal. Close to thirteen hundred British and U.S. bombers dropped 650,000 napalm (phosphorus) bombs onto Dresden. Since napalm cannot be extinguished and burns until everything is consumed, there was no hope for survival, especially in the inner city.

The first wave was launched on February 13, 1945, between 10:13 and 10:25 p.m.; the second wave, on February 14 from 1:22 to 1:54 a.m.; the third wave, from 12:15 to 12:25 p.m.; and a fourth wave on February 15 at daybreak finished the job. The first two attacks were carried out by British heavy bombers and the follow-up missions were carried out by their allies, the U.S. heavy bombers. In a matter of minutes, they unloaded tons of incendiary bombs on the heart of the city, its people, its thousands of refugees, and its baroque churches, famed opera house, and art museums.

The horrifying statistics relating to just this *one* mission in World War II against the city of Dresden read as follows: bombers: 1,295; bombs: 650,000; high explosives: 2,709 tons; and incendiaries:1,476 tons. Seventy percent of the city of Dresden was destroyed, and 135,000 people died (compared to 140,000 deaths in Hiroshima). In actuality, the number is probably higher, considering the never-ending stream of unknown refugees who had sought shelter in Dresden and the fact that most were incinerated beyond the point of recognition or identification, left in heaps of ashes. [7]

Using the Dresden soccer stadium as a reference point, British Lancasters and American Flying Fortresses dropped loads of napalm or white phosphorus bombs every fifty square yards out from this marker. The enormous flame that resulted was eight square miles wide, shooting smoke three miles high. For the next eighteen hours, regular bombs were dropped on top of this strange brew. Twenty-five minutes after the bombing, winds reached 150 miles an hour, sucking everything into the heart of the storm. Because the air became superheated and rushed upward, the fire lost most of its oxygen, creating tornadoes of flame that sucked the air right out of human lungs. The unfortunate ones who in desperation sought to escape the flames in the underground air-raid shelters either suffocated or were incinerated in waves of white heat. The city of Dresden burned for seven days and smoldered for weeks. [8]

Seventy percent of the Dresden dead either suffocated or died from poisonous gases that turned their bodies bright orange and blue. The intense heat melted some bodies into the pavement. People died by the thousands. The temperatures reached a thousand degrees or higher and melted glass. There was no escape for anyone caught in it.

Those who fled to the big park, the Grosse Garten (Great Garden), only prolonged the agony of those dreadful moments. Urged by auxiliary handheld public address systems (since all electric power had been lost), those who actually heard the warnings followed the advice and frantically ran, stumbled, or pushed their way to the park, which was still untouched. In the end, ten thousand of Dresden's citizens crowded into the Grosse Garten to escape the flames. In prewar times, the Grosse Garten had been a magnificent park nearly one and a half miles square and was enjoyed by so many citizens for strolls, to engage in social games, to listen to concerts, to visit the zoo, or just to appreciate nature in its splendor and beauty.

The planes returned at 1:22 a.m. to hit the Hauptbahnhof (main railroad station), which was still untouched, and the nearby park and zoo, killing the people who had sought refuge there. The attack came with no warning. There was a three-hour pause between the first and second raids. Twice as many bombers returned with a massive load of incendiary bombs. Utter panic struck the people.

The second wave was designed to concentrate on the Grosse Garten, as it had shown up on radar as a dark spot in the midst of the raging inferno. It was a complete "success." Within a few minutes, a sheet of flames ripped across the grass, uprooting some trees and littering the branches of others with everything from bicycles to human limbs. For days afterward, the debris remained bizarrely strewn about as grim reminders of Allied sadism.

A sad casualty and statistic was the Dresden Zoo, which was located within the Grosse Garten. The helpless animals, some quite exotic, did not stand a chance, and almost all suffered horrible deaths. Wild animals such as lions and tigers escaped from the broken enclosures of the zoo and ran into the terrified crowds. In their panic they attacked humans who were in the process of frantically running for safety themselves. Otto Sailer-Jackson was one of the keepers at Dresden Zoo on that fateful night of February 13th. He recalled that he faced the most difficult task when it became necessary and crucial to turn their attention to the carnivores. His words: "we did what we had to do, but it broke my heart". [9]

When it was over, the American planes finished the job by strafing (low flying, machine gunning) anything that moved on the ground, including a column of rescue vehicles rushing to the city to evacuate survivors and the many terrified Dresdners who rushed from the flames to the banks of the Elbe River.

The fourth attack concentrated its bomb load on the roads used by the fleeing population. When the last plane left the sky, Dresden was a scorched ruin, its blackened streets filled with corpses. The city was spared no horror. [10]

Ninety percent of the inner city, the most beautiful part of Dresden, was leveled (1,600 acres). Yet, inexplicably, some of the mansions on Wienerstrasse, which included my grandfather's home, were spared, although the railroad tracks that were always the main targets for Allied bombings were in close proximity. I checked a map of Dresden and discovered that Wienerstrasse runs parallel to the railroad tracks on one side and the Grosse Garten on the other. (Grandfather's home—see circle on map). The Hauptbahnhof, main railroad station, was only a few blocks away and was strategically and completely destroyed. How was our house missed? one might wonder.

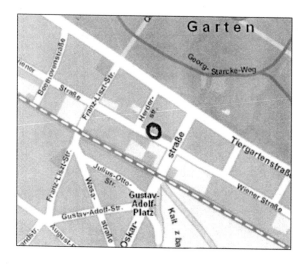

My father's two sisters, Tante Lis and Tante Gert, lived in that house until they had to vacate when a corporation took possession of this magnificent building. We learned this from my father, who, taking a tremendous risk, ventured into East Germany shortly after the war to revisit his father's home under the pretense of looking for his sisters. He was lucky that the Communist authorities did not suspect his being a former resident who had gotten away and was now living in the West.

Dresden and most of northern Germany had fallen under the Communist regime, and my father feared he might be discovered, arrested, or either killed or sent away to an undisclosed location within Russia, never to be heard from again. The Communists were brutal and were feared by all. All my father was able to surmise was that the beloved home of his father had been turned into an office building. He was devastated when he stood in front of the home of his childhood and saw what had become of it. The Communists had robbed this beautiful structure of its soul.

4

Life in Pulsnitz: 1939–1945

World War II started in September 1939, less than five months after I was born. I feel compelled to tell the story about my childhood and my experiences as I saw them. It is a very moving story that tells of the incredible courage and strength my mother possessed at a time when the entire country was in upheaval and human life meant very little to some and was the *only* thing that mattered to others. This precious gift of life—ours—was what my mother was determined to preserve, and this is what happened.

My early recollection of life in Pulsnitz near Dresden where we resided, is that of a normal childhood at first. I recall playing in the garden with my brothers Mike and Tom, going to town with my mother to buy groceries and always stopping at the *Lebkuchen* store (Pulsnitz was famous for its *Lebkuchen*, or gingerbread cakes), and visiting my mother's friend, whom we called Tante Hanni, who lived in an apartment on a small farm nearby.

One day when Mike and I went to visit Tante Hanni, an angry rooster attacked me. My screams alarmed both my aunt and the woman who owned and operated the farm. They quickly separated the rooster from my shoulders and hurried me, still hysterically screaming, inside. There, to my astonishment and I must say surprised pleasure, the woman gave me something syrupy, maybe honey. I was instantly distracted and delighted to have this sweet treat and calmed down. The incident must have been dramatic enough for me to remember it still to this day.

My brother Mike was three years older than I. He, therefore, was the first of us children to enter school. On his first day of school, as was customary in Germany, he was given his *Zuckertüte* (translated "sugar bag" or "sugar cone"), a cardboard cone about two feet long. It was decorated on the outside with a colorful design and filled with candy and chocolate to sweeten the "scary" first day of school for the new student. This custom is still in place in Germany today. To see those five-year-olds being brought to school on that frightful first day, proudly yet apprehensively clutching their *Zuckertüte*, is a charming and heartwarming sight to all those adults who once held one themselves. Since I was the sibling next in line, and my brother Tom after me, we were each given a smaller *Zuckertüte* as a consolation. Mine was about one foot long, and Tom, the youngest among us, held his between two fingers. We were so pleased and happy; after all, school was not beckoning us just yet!

*Mike's first day of school
(standing next to his teacher, Mr. Kilian)*

I believe my sister Sabine had not yet been born. That happy event took place in November 1944. Mutti was rushed to the nearby hospital. Her sister Alice, or Tante Ali to us, was by her side. My father was not there but came home on a brief military paternity leave shortly thereafter.

We children were allowed to visit Mutti and our new sister in the hospital. I have fond memories of seeing my mother, and next to her in a bassinet was a baby, my sister. Mutti motioned for us to reach under the blanket of this baby and take out the little gift our new sister had brought along. Oh, what a joy! We loved her right away. She had come such a long way— from where, we had no idea—and yet she had thought of us with a gift! This was special indeed.

Tom, maybe three years old, decided one day while my mother was still in the hospital to set out to visit Mutti and the baby. He sneaked out of the house without being noticed by our nanny. He actually made it and walked right into the hospital, where he was stopped and questioned by the nursing staff. They quickly understood where he intended to go and led him up the stairs to the room he was looking for.

A day or so later, Tom and Mike went together. On the way back home from the hospital, they came upon an apple orchard. They saw those apples and, though the apples were very green, ate them. It was a great idea at the time because they were hungry, but it made them gravely ill and we almost lost them.

When Tom and I visited Pulsnitz in 1994, we went to the hospital, which was under active reconstruction at that time. Tom did peek inside the hospital briefly (not to disturb the construction workers) and recognized those stairs he had climbed trying to get to our mother and our newborn sister. We then turned around to walk back to our car; on the way, we came upon the apple orchard, and Tom cringed.

It was a very carefree childhood. We played in our yard with a swing, not the elaborate swing set of nowadays but just one single swing, and we were content to share it happily. We exchanged visits with our neighbor's kids through a hole in the fence between our two homes, which was created by no other than my brother Mike. We built tents in the garden with Tante Ali, Mutti's sister, and stood naked in an aluminum tub placed outside to get hosed down on hot days. We helped Mutti pick berries from the bushes in our yard and later noticed the many glass jars in our basement containing canned vegetables, fruits, and jams.

Once, I recall, we all took a train ride to Dresden to meet Tante Lis, my father's older sister. Strangely, the only thing I remember from our visit to that beautiful city was a very large square with a beautiful, imposing building. Having gone back to Dresden in 1994, I realize this must have been the state opera house, Semper Opera, where one of our ancestors, Eduard Schmidt-Decarli, sang in the late 1800s.

It was a very normal childhood, it would seem, as seen through the eyes of a child. An interesting recollection is that my brother Mike sometime in 1944 joined what he thought was the Hitler Jugend (Hitler Youth). Mike was very proud of his uniform and gleefully attended the meetings with his best friend, Mrs. Gellner's son, who lived next door. In retrospect, he probably wore the Jung Volk (Young People) uniform, which was the precursor for the Hitler Jugend that was mandatory for boys aged ten to fourteen. In my recollection, the uniform consisted of short pants, a beige shirt, and a scarf. Since Mike was only eight years old, I conclude that it was probably more likely the Jung Volk uniform. Boy Scouts no longer existed in Germany at that time.

Although scouting was abolished by the Nazis upon seizing power in 1933, they nevertheless adopted the militaristic features of scouting and expanded them in the Hitler Jugend program. It's an unfortunate fact of history that when Hitler consolidated youth groups in Germany, he chose to keep many of the trappings of the scouts for the Hitler Youth. As a result, years later, traditional American scouting practices such as saluting the flag, standing at attention for flag raising and lowering, and using a ranking system remain absent in today's German scouting because they don't want to be associated with the military. [11]

Mike's group met a few times in the school yard across the street from our house, and that was that. I never asked my mother about it, so it is hard to put things together now. His association with this particular group was of relatively short duration.

Thinking back, my brother's joining at the young age of eight could have been the idea of Mrs. Gellner next door, whose husband was very involved in a German government agency and whose son, Mike's best friend, had already joined the Jung Volk. Knowing Mutti, she could not have come up with this unless she had been pressured by other circumstances; that is, my brother's youthful exuberance influenced by his best friend's example. It is also possible that Mrs. Gellner herself suggested it and could have viewed Mutti as unpatriotic and reported her to the authorities if she had not been willing to have her son participate. Mutti had to be careful; there were snitches all around. People were hauled off by the SS (Schutzstaffel, the protective echelon for the Führer) or the Gestapo (secret police), sometimes in the middle of the night, and were never seen again, all because a neighbor or so-called friend had tipped them off. Even teachers used students to innocently tell on their parents. A time of all-around fear gripped the German population.

Food was hard to come by, and Mutti had to perform wonders feeding her family. There was a morning when news traveled around town that the neighborhood bakery had suffered a fire the night before and the owners of the bakery had invited all residents to come and get free of charge whatever bread was left, as they certainly could not sell it. We too went to obtain our bread. As we stepped into the store, we were greeted by the overwhelming stench of cold, water-soaked cinders, and the lingering smoke took our breath away. The bread smelled and tasted of smoke and fire, almost resembling toast but more intensely so. I can still taste it in my mind—not pleasant at all. But we ate it just the same. After all, bread was bread.

Then, as I became aware of it, I sensed that my mother was bothered and worried about something my little innocent mind could not attempt to imagine. There were also strange people living in our upstairs rooms, such as German army nurses and then later a high-ranking officer who was attached to the units of wounded soldiers in the schoolhouse across the street (explanation to follow).

I also recall that my father was not with us; he visited us on only a few occasions. At those times, he was always dressed in German military uniform when he first arrived. Did he change into civilian clothes during his military leave? I doubt it. Not honoring the uniform could have been considered treason and he could have been arrested by the authorities, as it was done to so many German citizens for the slightest reasons in those days. Besides, Mutti must have also told him of her suspicions about Mrs. Gellner next door; he understood.

Danger to the average citizen lurked from within as well as from forces on the outside. An inadvertent anti-government expression or misconception, not saluting or "heiling" ("Heil, Hitler"), or simply not acting in a required way could mark you an enemy of the *Führer* and cause you to be led away.

On those few occasions when my father came home on military leave, my mother was always visibly delighted and relieved to see him, but she cried when he left again.

And then it began: the wailing sirens that announced danger from the air and caused all citizens to seek shelter. My first experience was while I was in kindergarten, when the sirens sounded and the teachers very quickly and force-fully, I thought, hurried us into the underground bunker where we sat for a while. The adults were all looking towards the ceiling in anticipation, it seemed, of something dreadful to happen. We children had no idea why we were there, but the adults apparently did. This "exercise" was repeated daily and occurred more often until it was a constant.

One day my brother Mike and I were on our way home from *Kindergarten* (for me) and *Kinderhort* for Mike, who was three years older, when the sirens started. Both of us did not know what to do. What was happening? There were no adults to tell us where to go and how to behave. We also had no idea why the sirens were sounding in the first place. So in our confusion, we picked a big tree and huddled underneath it. Then we heard the sound of the planes above. The oh-so-eerie hum of multiple plane engines still rings in my ears to this day. We were too young to know the intense danger we were in; we figured that the tree would hide us just fine.

We were quickly grabbed and hurried away by neighbors who had seen us, and again we were ushered into an underground shelter. This time it was more apparent. We actually heard the impact of the explosions, though we did not know that they were bombs and somehow connected to the roaring planes above and that they caused death and destruction wherever they hit. We sensed the horror around us. We waited until the sirens sounded again, this time in a different pitch to signal that the danger was over and everybody was allowed to surface again. Without hesitation, we hurried home into the safety of our mother's arms.

The air raids were not limited to daytime but continued through the night. This meant that several times during the night when the sirens "sang their awful, spine-chilling song", my mother would come upstairs, take the youngest of her four children (Tom and Sabine), and urge Mike and me to hurry on downstairs where we would huddle in the basement, oddly enough, surrounded by all those shelves with canned fruits and vegetables. As it turned out, we never consumed any of it. We heard the planes above—that awful roaring sound!—and by then Mike and I had started to realize that this was not fun and games the grown-ups had dreamt up, but that we were in very serious danger.

According to my mother's description, I seemed to have been the child who had this realization first and took it the hardest. My sunny disposition, for which I was adored even by our pediatrician, suddenly disappeared. My curly hair went straight almost overnight, and I would simply collapse when urged to get out of bed and hurry down to the basement after so many air raids a night. And so my dear mother had to carry me downstairs as well. My legs just didn't hold me up any longer.

Where are our smiles?

As I learned later, the planes we heard roaring above were the Allied planes, in particular British and later American, who apparently at one point had the mission in the winter of 1945 to destroy cities in northern Germany like Berlin, Leipzig, Jena, Chemnitz, and finally Dresden. Actually, the night flights were initially conducted by the Royal Air Force, while the U.S. bombers stuck to a slightly more humane policy of daylight precision bombing concentrating on military, industrial, and manufacturing structures. Later they joined their British allies in the execution of nighttime area bombing campaigns of civilian targets in Germany, better known as "saturation bombing" or "moral bombing." A question comes to mind here: what *moral* parameters were they using when the decision was made to attack in such a manner? Pardon my cynicism.

Down below, where we were in the more rural areas, we quickly understood the looming danger, and homes were equipped with blackout shades to be drawn on all windows so that we could not be spotted from the air at night. Even bicycles with dynamo-powered lights and cars were instructed to drive with only a sliver of a light beam pointed downward. Naturally, an entire city like Dresden could not be blacked out, nor did its residents expect to be bombed at this stage of the war, especially since Dresden had been declared a safe city. But it soon became apparent that nothing and no one was safe in the end. The planes aimed at everything that was lit up at night or that moved during the day. The saturation bombardment of "Bomber" Harris and his U.S. counterparts on major cities in Germany resulted in hundreds of thousands of innocent dead German civilians, mostly women, children, and older people. The able men, like my father, had been inducted into the military and sent to the Front; they had no choice.

War is a terrible thing. Fear, despair, and devastating losses are experienced on all fronts. This is the story of terror experienced by just one family—our family. On either side of conflict, one finds vulnerable human beings caught up in the upheaval of war and its consequences. The other side lives in fear and anguish, degradation, deprivation, hunger, and tears. How many innocent lives were lost altogether on both sides? One can only shudder.

My mother made a poignant comment about the folly of war when she stated, "Politicians start wars—not civilians." Called up for combat, men dutifully set out to battle. Most men are not particularly political, but rather focused on the well-being and safety of their families. They obediently set out to battle, leaving loving families behind who pray to God for their safe return. Ironically, the families of the opposing combatants are praying to the same God for their loved ones' protection. God must be troubled.

At one point during this unsettling time, my mother and her neighbor, Frau Gellner, who lived with her three children in the adjacent part of our duplex home, decided to create a connection between the two homesteads by punching a huge hole through the fire wall in the basement large enough for people to fit through so that if it became necessary, our families could traverse from one side to the other. I remember seeing that hole after its completion and my mother's explanation what it was for. Somewhat puzzled and with a child's logic, I thought it odd, as we could have just walked from our front door to theirs in order to visit.

This hole, as it turned out, could have saved the family that moved into our house in February 1945 after my mother and Frau Gellner with altogether seven kids decided to leave on the last train out of town. Unfortunately, the poor refugee family that accepted my mother's gracious and generous offer to move into our house didn't know of its existence and thus perished.

Where were we that fateful night of February 13–14? That night the sirens sounded almost continuously. The droning noise in the air seemed eerily different from all the other air raid sounds we were somehow accustomed to—as if you could ever get used to it. To this day, more than sixty years later, this sound still gives me the chills. The sound that night came from hundreds of British and American heavy bombers in the night sky.

Our small town of Pulsnitz was in their flight path, as the planes, rather than making a direct approach, circled around Dresden not to be detected. A calculated surprise attack was in the making. Once the air raids began, the sirens in our town wailed continuously throughout the night and intensified into the following day.

Some of our neighbors who did not have a basement came rushing over to join us and huddled with us. My mother had already dragged us children down to the basement several times that night, and we sat there listening in horror and fright to the never-ending roar of planes above. As I learned later, they were on their way to Dresden. This went on for hours until we heard the sound of the sirens in their specific pitch to signal that it was finally over, at least for that night.

The adults went upstairs first, and I followed. I will never forget my puzzlement at what I saw when I joined my mother and our neighbors on the raised stoop outside our front door. When I immerged, I was startled by an unexpected brightness all around us. Everyone seemed to be very upset; some were crying, and all were looking and pointing towards a particular point on the horizon. The sky had turned into an intense orange-yellow, and this brightness seemed to dome over one spot—Dresden. What puzzled me in particular was the fact that I knew in my little heart that it was the middle of the night, so why was everything so bright? Dresden had been burning for hours.

When it was all over, there were only ruins and ashes and 135,000 dead civilians, not to mention the immeasurable loss of art and architecture. Good-bye to a great city in all its splendor and the great people who had been its inhabitants, as were once our grandparents, relatives, and friends before this dreadful war. The town of Pulsnitz is located only 15 miles northeast of Dresden, just far enough away not to have been physically affected by the attack on Dresden eight years after my parents left that city to settle in Pulsnitz.

Gerhart Hauptmann, Poet and 1912 Nobel Prize Laureate for Literature, proclaimed in 1945 "He who has forgotten how to cry, will relearn it again by the sight of the fallen city of Dresden".

Tante Lis, my father's older sister, wrote to my sister Sabine many years later and described the turmoil and uncertainty of the time just prior to and the week following the attacks on Dresden. According to my mother's description, backed up by this letter from my aunt, Tante Lis was worried sick over whether my mother had actually made it to Dresden on the day of the first air raid on this great city. According to their previous plans, my mother was to take all her children to Dresden on that day to meet up with Tante Lis so they could be together as a family during this trying time of fear and despair.

Tante Lis's letter is handwritten in old German script, not easily decipherable, but either Sabine or I will attempt to translate it at one point and include it in this document. Apparently, what really happened was that my mother did not go to Dresden on that day (intuition or other fateful guidance?). Then the air raids on Dresden were unleashed. Immediately after, my mother was urged by the military officer who lived in our house to prepare to leave our home at the next possible opportunity. She did not have the time or means to communicate this to Tante Lis, who lived in Pappritz just 5 miles east of Dresden.

Tante Lis wrote that she was so desperate to find out what had happened to us that she decided to set out on foot in freezing February rain and snow to go to Pulsnitz herself, only to find that we were no longer there. Her heart sank; now she thought for sure we had gone to Dresden as discussed and gotten caught in the awful firestorm there. But after many inquiries, she was told that we had left town on the last Red Cross train and allowed another family to live in our house. Weeks later she learned that we were in Bavaria. We were alive!

My mother's decision to flee our hometown in February 1945 after the attack on Dresden no doubt saved our lives. We probably would not have survived the fire that was set by the Russians as they entered our town unless my mother remembered the hole in the wall in the basement and could have taken us to the other side. She certainly spared us living under the brutality of the Russians with their vicious attacks in drunken stupor on women and children for the remainder of 1945 and the oppressive Soviet regime that followed.

When my father visited Dresden shortly after the war, he also went to Pulsnitz, our birthplace, which by then had become part of East Germany. There he saw the burnt-out homestead at Kuehnstrasse. He also looked up Hanni Faust, my parents' friend and neighbor who had remained in Pulsnitz through the Russians' takeover of our town. Hanni had also witnessed the burning of our home from a block away.

My father learned that when the town of Pulsnitz was in the process of undergoing postwar cleanup, Hanni came upon several workers who were having lunch outside our former home. One of them was eating out of one of the two Chinese dragon Meissen wall plates that originally were displayed in the old residence at Wienerstrasse in Dresden and then at Kuehnstrasse in Pulsnitz. The worker found this Meissen plate still hanging at the chimney wall in what used to be our living room. She explained to the worker the importance and sentimental value this plate held for our family, and without hesitation he handed it to her. Hanni gladly presented this plate to my father during his postwar visit.

This plate (dating back to 1734) having survived the fire at Kuehnstrasse is now hanging on my dining room wall; mine is the gray dragon, while my sister Sabine has the red dragon, which somehow was recovered through my father's brother Robert with the help of his sister, Tante Lis (Luise).

5

Resurrection from Ashes

When my brother Tom and I visited Dresden in 1994 after the reunification, there was a tremendous amount of reconstruction in progress. Nothing had been touched during the East German-Soviet regime. Buildings had stood in ruin for over forty-five years. When it was decided to resurrect the city of Dresden, any building or structure that was stable and representative of the city's past up to 1945 was restored rather than demolished.

And so you could see facades that showed two-tone brick: yellow, representing the new brick; black, the old burnt brick. Not even sandblasting could get the black out of the stone. It was quite shocking to see this reminder of an awful occurrence. Even the stone bridge over the Elbe River, which has quite a span, was blackened and still is; we could not believe it. We watched in amazement how the mutilated statues and figurines that had originally crowned the royal courtyard of the Zwinger were diligently repaired and replicated by skilled craftsmen and were in the process of being readied to be placed back onto the pedestals from which they had toppled. It was sheer artistry at work.

The famous Semper Opera near this bridge was painstakingly restored to its original architectural splendor, but one could see the two-tone effect on this beautiful structure as well. Tom and I were especially touched, as we knew that our great-grandfather, Eduard Schmidt Decarli (1846–1903), had been a member (baritone) of the famed Dresden opera under the stage name Decarli. Thus my mother's documented name was Elsie Emilie Schmidt-Decarli.

"Kings are rendered immortal by their buildings"— this was the motto of Augustus II (Augustus the Strong, 1670–1733), elector of Saxony and king of Poland, when he approved construction of the Dresdner Frauenkirche in 1726. Regretfully, this magnificent structure had become a casualty of the air raids in 1945 as well.

An absolute wonder of ingenuity and modern technology was the literal resurrection of the Frauenkirche (Church of Our Lady) in Dresden, a structure of beauty and unusual stature. The church was originally built between 1726 and 1743 as a Lutheran cathedral by George Baehr, Dresden's city architect, although Saxony's prince-elector, Frederick August I, was Catholic. On December 2, 1736, Johann Sebastian Bach performed a recital on the magnificent Silbermann organ in a dedicatory concert. Playing for two hours in the still-unfinished sanctuary, Bach pronounced both the instrument and hall to be near perfect acoustically.

The main body of this beautiful church was originally topped with a ninety-six-meter tall dome. The dome had no internal supports and was compared to the construction of the dome at St. Peter's Basilica in Rome. The twelve-thousand-ton sandstone dome stood high, resting remarkably on eight slender pillars. During those two fateful February nights and days in 1945, the church withstood the repeated air attacks, and the eight pillars supporting the large dome held up long enough for the evacuation of three hundred people who had sought shelter in the church crypt before succumbing to the immense heat created by the repeated napalm bombings. As mentioned earlier, the temperature around and inside the church reached a thousand degrees Celsius.[12] The dome finally collapsed at 10:00 a.m. on February 15. The pillars glowed bright red and exploded; the outer walls shattered, and nearly six thousand tons of stone plunged to earth, penetrating the massive floor as it fell.

Tom and I saw with our own eyes how little of this magnificent architecture actually remained standing. The two fractions of the outer walls of the main body of the church were painful to one's eye and heart. All around there was just rubble. Initially, the altar and chancel still stood among the rubble. After the reunification of Germany, they became part of the reconstruction efforts. Two thousand pieces of the original altar were cleaned and incorporated into the new structure.

A sign was placed on the protective fence around the reconstruction site of the Frauenkirche which read: "Bruecken bauen (build Bridges) – Versoehnung leben (live Reconciliation)".

In January of 1993, the archaeological cleanup of the ruin was started. Approximately twenty-six thousand tons of rubble and stone needed to be sorted, photographed, numbered, and placed on shelves next to the church in a fenced-in, well-protected area. Hundreds of architects, art historians, and engineers sorted thousands of stones, identifying and labeling each for reuse in the new structure. With very sophisticated virtual reality computer technology using the original blueprints and photographs, this church was brought back to its original appearance—an unbelievable endeavor!

History of Reconstruction

On November 24, 1989, ten citizens of Dresden began the initiative to rebuild the church. There was some reservation at first amongst the Dresdners, since the ruin had in the meantime become a formidable monument and reminder of the effects of war. Popular sentiment discouraged the authorities from clearing the ruins to make room for a parking lot. In 1966, the remnants had been officially declared a "memorial against war," and state-controlled commemorations were held there on the anniversaries of the destruction of Dresden.

Support for rebuilding increased rapidly. In February 1990, a worldwide appeal for support, known as the Call from Dresden, was launched. The response from around the world, which included the British and Americans whose attacks had destroyed the city in 1945, as well as private donors from amongst Dresden residents and throughout Germany who purchased individual building stones, was resounding. The names of all donors, regardless of size of contribution, are now inscribed in the church's historical registry.

The following facts deserve mention to reveal the remarkable *international* effort towards reconstruction that took place all those years later.

Günter Blobel, a German-born American, had seen the church as a boy when his family fled from Silesia to escape the advancing Red Army, passing through Dresden and then taking shelter in a town just outside of Dresden days before the city was bombed. In 1994, he became the founder and president of the nonprofit Friends of Dresden, Inc., a United States organization dedicated to supporting the reconstruction, restoration, and preservation of Dresden's artistic and architectural legacy. In 1999, he won the Nobel Prize in Medicine and donated the entire amount of his award money of nearly one million dollars to the organization for the restoration of Dresden, to the rebuilding of the Frauenkirche and the building of a new synagogue. It was the single largest individual donation to the project.

In Great Britain, Dr. Paul Oestreicher, a canon emeritus of Coventry Cathedral and founder of the Dresden Trust in 1993, wrote, "The church (Frauenkirche) is to Dresden what St. Paul's (Cathedral) is to London. This is true both architecturally and psychologically".[13] The fund raised six hundred thousand £ pounds from two thousand people and a hundred companies and trusts in Britain. Among the curators of the trust were the Duke of Kent as its royal patron and the bishop of Coventry.

Additional organizations included France's Association Frauenkirche Paris and Switzerland's Verein Schweizer Freunde der Frauenkirche.

Dresdner Bank financed more than half of the reconstruction costs via a donor-certificates campaign, collecting almost seventy million euros after 1995. The bank itself contributed more than seven million euros, including more than one million donated by its employees.

The new gilded eight-meter orb and cross on top of the dome were forged by Grant Macdonald Silversmiths in London using the original eighteenth-century techniques as much as possible, even using medieval nails recovered from the ruins of the roof of Coventry Cathedral. It was constructed by Alan Smith, a British goldsmith from London whose father, Frank, was a member of one of the aircrews that took part in the bombing of Dresden. In February 2000, the cross was ceremonially handed over by the Duke of Kent to be placed on top of the dome. The cross that once topped the dome, now twisted and charred, stands to the right of the new altar.

It was decided not to produce a replica of the original Silbermann organ. This decision caused a short-lived public dispute known as the Dresden Organ Strike. In the end, a new 4,873-pipe organ was built by Daniel Kern of Strasbourg, France, and was completed in April 2005.

Total cost for reconstruction was over $220 million, with an extensive team of architects and historians utilizing the original blueprints and original stones. Let us not forget the international involvement, as described above. Isn't it heartwarming to see former adversaries coming together to make a wrong right?

The first religious service and reopening ceremony given in the new church in October of 2005 was a very moving tearjerker. The Dresdners had their church back, their heart and their soul. At the reopening festivities and religious service, many dignitaries from around the world were in attendance, including a delegation from Great Britain and the United States. As the crowd gathered inside as well as outside the church during the service, the sentiment of reconciliation could be felt all around. There is hope for humanity after all.

And yes, Albert Christoph Bierling's statue of Martin Luther was restored and set atop its base on the original site in front of the Frauenkirche.

There is a similar story to be told. Among the many German cities that were likewise attacked and destroyed by the Allies was Berlin, which was bombed repeatedly from 1943 to 1945 and was left with immense rubble and destruction that included the remains of their beloved church Gedaechtniskirche at the top end of Kurfürstendamm, which was then and still is today the central shopping avenue of Berlin. The remains basically consisted of the torched and pockmarked spire that rose from the rubble of what used to be the main body of the church. Here too, the proud Berliners insisted on keeping the tower as it stood as a reminder of the destruction of Berlin and their desperate hours of fear and loss, but also as a reminder of their will to rebuild.

The voices of the Berliners were steadfast, and finally it was decided to build a new modern body of the church right next to the stump of the old church tower. Although in the end no one really was enthralled with the modern architecture that joined the old leftover church, the deliberate reminder does make the desired statement. It stands like this today and has become a formidable landmark for Berlin, a stark contrast to the modern architecture that emerged from the rubble all around as the reconstruction began in 1959 and was completed in 1961.

6

A Flight for Life

B ack to 1945: As I mentioned before, my father came
home to visit us a few times during his military duty
in the German Air Force, the Luftwaffe. I have stored his
service record in a large binder; it reveals all the assignments
and military leaves that were granted to him. One of those
home visits was for the birth of the last of his four children,
my sister Sabine in November 1944. That was the last time
we saw him before our odyssey began.

The winter of 1944–45 was horrible. I remember walking
with my mother to town one wintry day to get groceries.
The entire stretch of road was lined with horse-drawn flatbed
wagons, some of them canvas covered, like wagons in the
Old West, and all loaded with personal belongings and carrying families with people of all ages, from grandparents to
the smallest baby. I was told later that some of those babies
froze to death in their wet diapers and skimpy clothing and
as a result of malnutrition.

These people were refugees from regions farther north
and east of our area and had been on the move for days,
some for weeks. They had been forced to leave their homes
at a moment's notice and were desperately fleeing from the
Russian front, which was rapidly closing in on their home-

land, Poland, Prussia, Lithuania, Silesia, and Pomerania, streaming towards Dresden. The Russians were truly barbaric, raping and pilfering as they advanced through the towns. Entire villages, inhabited mostly by defenseless women and children and the elderly, were wiped out, as the able men were away, enlisted into a war they did not want. This was certainly true of my father. The families that managed to get away early just left their homes and headed west and south with one single thought in mind: to save their lives. I will tell you about our encounter with just one such refugee family momentarily.

Across the street from our house on Kuehnstrasse was a school building with a very big school yard and a huge gymnasium. This gym was utilized to temporarily accommodate all the wounded German soldiers who were brought into our town continually throughout the winter of 1944–45. Because of the overcrowding of the Red Cross facilities in Dresden, surrounding towns such as Pulsnitz were asked to take in the wounded and refugees fleeing the Russian advance.

The wounded soldiers who were sent to our town were lying in the school gymnasium on the cold hardwood floor, lined up like sardines. My older brother Mike and I went over to the school many times to visit these soldiers. I remember my favorite one was a young man, though to me he seemed rather old at the time, who had red hair and seemingly millions of red freckles. I tried to count them, but at the age of five, I did not get very far. The soldier chuckled in amusement and watched me as I struggled on.

According to my mother, the commanding officer attached to the troops in the school gym lived in our house during that time. He apparently knew more about the status and turn of events of the war, especially after the destruction of Dresden. One evening in February 1945, just days afterwards, he told my mother that if she did not get out of town the next day, there would be no hope for us. He knew that on the next day the very last train would leave the town of Pulsnitz, carrying all the wounded soldiers, including my freckle-faced redhead, and heading somewhere—anywhere—away from the war zone.

We could already hear the explosions in the distance, telling us that the Russians were moving in our direction. That was bad news! The Americans were the threat from the air and the Russians on the ground. Where was one to hide? The only thing to do was to flee. Now we found ourselves in the same hopeless and fearful situation as all those refugees from the Baltic countries north of us who had left everything behind and fled south, coming through our town earlier.

And so the next morning, we kids were rather surprised when my mother dressed us warmly in layers and placed a fully packed knapsack on each of our backs. Where did she get those little knapsacks on such short notice? I have no clue and regretfully never made it a point later to ask my mother. She took the baby carriage for my sister, who was only three months old, and stuffed a meager food supply into the sides of the carriage around her. She also took the packed-to-the-rim black travel trunk that belonged to my father.

This trunk was like a portable closet. It had drawers as well as racks for hanging clothing items. This black trunk, bearing the initials A. B. for Alfred Bierling, my father, is now in my possession and stands in my laundry room. There is nothing stored in it. I just don't have the heart to discard this witness to a crucial time in our past. I have never seen another trunk like this in all my years.

As described above, besides warm clothing for the entire family, my mother took my sister's powdered formula, which was called Alete-Milch, and four staple food items for the rest of us: dry rolled oats, milk powder, cocoa powder, sugar—that's all! These food items would keep us alive during the next two weeks.

There was one other item my mother just could not leave behind; it was our nameplate on our garden gate, which my parents had brought along from Dresden in 1936. That brass nameplate moved with us from place to place—even to the United States—and is now proudly displayed on the entry pillar to my brother Tom's home in Long Island.

Our leaving is a moving, unforgettable story. The day of our departure was bitterly cold and snowy. Shortly before we were ready to leave our house, I observed my mother talking to a family outside our front gate. I still see them: all huddled in shawls and blankets, seemingly feeling cold and weary, without hope or home. It was one of those families on the move described earlier in my story. At one point, their faces seemed to light up; my mother apparently had told them that we were leaving and that they could move into our house, make themselves comfortable, and eat all the food that was available, including the many jars of canned fruit and vegetables lined up on shelves in our basement. Yes, it was the same basement we had cowered in during those frightful nights of air raids.

And so, as this family of strangers filed into our house— children, parents, grandparents— my mother pushed the baby carriage with my sister and urged her three other children along our front-yard walkway and out through the gate one last time. We were on our way to the railroad station to catch that last train out of town, and with that we became one of those refugee families on the move to nowhere—just like that!

A sad after-note regarding the family that so thankfully moved into our house: we later learned from Tante Hanni, who remained in Pulsnitz, that they perished in our house, just the same. When the Russians came into our town, they randomly picked certain homes and placed gasoline-drenched rags inside them while holding the people hostage at gunpoint and then set the rags on fire. When "our" poor family tried to run outside to escape the flames, they were all shot to death. The Russians were actually waiting for them, as if it were an arcade game!

So on that bitter cold and snowy morning in February of 1945, my mother pushed the baby carriage with my sister through the snow, followed by her other three bewildered and scared small children who were weighted down with fully packed knapsacks, and aimed in the direction of the railroad station. How ingenious was my mother? The wheels of the carriage actually had little skis attached; otherwise, the task of pushing the baby carriage through the heavy snow would have been impossible.

I believe the rather large black trunk was taken to the station by the officer who lived with us. I am sure it was also that same officer who secured a place on the train for us, since you couldn't buy a ticket. You had to fend for yourself and get permission, but from whom? Every family was left to their own devices. I guess the pull of a military officer was sufficient for my mother and her flock.

Frau Gellner, our immediate neighbor back at Kuehnstrasse, apparently had no worries either, as her husband had great influence in the local German government. I wouldn't be surprised if it was the SS. We learned later that the entire Gellner family went back to East Germany after the war ended, and all were active in the Communist Party. Why was my mother not surprised?

From the moment we set out on our odyssey, I recall my mother wearing a head scarf over her hair, neatly folded in a certain way as was done by so many women then. In its completed stage, the folded head cover took on an oblong appearance, successfully enveloping the wearer's hair. My mother wore it almost the entire time we were on that horrible train ride to God-only-knew-where and occasionally thereafter.

As mentioned, my brother Tom and I went back to that railroad station in June of 1994. As we walked through the echoing halls of this station house (the large station clock and luggage scale were still there), we imagined how our mother must have felt when she arrived there almost fifty years earlier, having left her beloved home on Kuehnstrasse and not knowing where we were going and what danger was lurking ahead. She had no time to hesitate or wonder; she had to protect four children, and her husband was far away. Her mother-hen instinct gave her the courage and strength to bravely and daringly forge into a very risky undertaking.

I would like to pass on a quote I heard that struck me deeply when it was recited during church service recently. The truth it contains was stunning as it applies to my mother's moment of fateful decision in February 1945, as well as all choices that she had to make in the years that followed:

Courage is fear that has heard God speak and has asked for His presence and power.

Once on the train, we were allotted one compartment to share with another family, ironically, Frau Gellner and her three children. Each family was granted the use of one bench. A straw mattress lay between the two benches and was to be shared by both families. Ah, what a treat to sleep lying down rather than sitting up and leaning against either your mother or one of your siblings who was leaning back on you! My mother never lay down but sat up for the entire two weeks, with my three-month-old sister Sabine either resting beside her or on her lap. Besides quarreling with the kids on the opposite bench over whose turn it was to sleep on the straw mattress, there was one other rather unpleasant thing we had to endure. Even at our young age, we felt rather uncomfortable waiting for the potty to be handed around and having to sit there in front of everyone. Now as I am recalling this, I am wondering, what did the grown-ups do? My mother?

One of the clothing items my mother also brought along was a sleeveless fur jacket. She kept my sister's formula warm by storing the bottles under the jacket close to her body. Once in a while, this fur jacket was handed around so we could warm our bodies for a few minutes before handing it on to one of our siblings and then back to our mother. The treasured fur jacket—actually, it was a vest—lasted for many years thereafter. I really can't remember when it finally outlived its usefulness, but I do recall my parents sharing this garment for a long time.

The train ride over the next two weeks was very similar to the train ride shown in the movie *Dr. Zhivago* many, many years later, though the movie depicted the Russian revolution rather than World War II. The human experience and drama, however, is always the same, no matter in what time period it is played out. When my mother saw the movie, she shivered, remembering her own ordeal many years past.

The train moved only at night, with blackout shades drawn on every window so we would not be spotted from the air. During the day, the train usually stopped in a wooded area, again so as not to be seen from above. The Allied planes were known to destroy railroad tracks and moving trains. I did not know at that time that we the Germans had started the war and were the enemy and needed to be stopped and destroyed. From the Allied viewpoint, any train could be transporting the supply line of either ammunition or military equipment or personnel. Unfortunately, war does not distinguish between political or military forces and a mother with her four children sitting on a train, hoping to stay alive.

Each time the train stopped, my mother quickly ran to the locomotive up front to get hot water for my sister's formula and to mix our staple food. (Remember the rolled oats, powdered milk, cocoa, and sugar?) She also never missed a chance to drop off a postcard to my father's field number to tell him that we had left home and were now in such and such town. I do remember it well; every stop on the way, my mother grabbed that one-handle pot and hurried out of our train compartment. For her it was always the same routine: locomotive for hot water and then on to the station house to drop off the postcard to my father.

On one of those days when my mother was inside the station house to deposit her postcard, she turned to check on the train and realized with horror that it was moving out of the station. *Her children were on that train!* She ran after the train, never letting go of the pot of hot water she had just fetched, and caught up with the train and ran alongside it, trying to figure out how to jump onto it. She wasn't going to let her children disappear!

The last wagon approached quickly, and with her last strength, she grabbed the handrail that extended near the wagon door and swung herself onto the running board (how ironic), still holding on to the pot, from which the water was long gone, as it was the only pot she had. She clung to the board with death-defying determination and cried in anger and frustration until she realized that her tears had frozen to her face. The wind howled across her body as the train picked up speed. She endured this horrendous experience with almost supernatural strength and persistence, and when the train came to a halt at the next town, she peeled herself off the board and quickly came to check on us, her children, who were too small to realize what had just happened. I don't think my mother left a postcard in that particular town, and I was told that one of the other mothers on the train got the water the next few times for all of us to share. My mother had some recuperating to do, and besides, she was not going to let us out of her sight again so quickly.

Some families decided to get off the train at stations along the way, at towns like Eisenach or Hof, which, they supposed, were a safe distance from Dresden and other war-torn areas in northern Germany. This proved to be a fatal mistake, as the Russians came to those towns shortly thereafter and massacred most of them. Mutti, thank God, thought it wiser to stay on the train to gain more distance. Once again, she saved our lives.

Finally, one late afternoon some two weeks later, the train stopped at a small town in Bavaria: Neumarkt St. Veit. Here we were all told to get out. We were gathered in the station hall and given some food by the Red Cross (Rote Kreuz). The food, I recall, was a watery bread soup, weak broth with bread pieces swimming in it. But it was warm—no, it was hot—and that was our first really hot meal in two weeks. We could even warm our hands on the bowl—how wonderful!

According to my mother, a Red Cross nurse from town came over to us and took my little sister right out of my mother's arms and walked away. In horror, my mother dashed after her only to find out that the nurse merely wanted to give my little sister a bath. And so little three-month-old Sabine received her first bath in two weeks, a change of clothes, and formula served at a more baby-appropriate temperature. My mother was in tears with gratitude.

A thought comes to my mind after all this time: God bless the train operators in whose hands our lives rested throughout those two weeks! Any move the train made was at their discretion and at extraordinary risk. Traveling at night without using any light source whatsoever must have been an impossible task. I distinctly recall that we had to draw down blackout shades on every window each night. How could the train operators be sure that the tracks we were traveling on were still intact? And how were they able to find a wooded area just in time before daybreak to hide in its cover? I am sure that when we reached the final destination, Neumarkt St. Veit, everyone was so confused and insecure about what was going to happen next that no one thought of thanking the train operator and his crew for what they had done for us. May I do this now, in the name of all those who were saved through their heroic and selfless actions.

Our first night in a real bed after that awful train ride was in a large hall of the Red Cross rescue facility in Neumarkt St. Veit. Here is where I saw my first bunk bed. Since I was the second oldest, I was allowed to sleep on one of the top bunks. The next morning brought a scary surprise: we were visited by military police, probably German, as it is quite possible that they were the same military personnel who had traveled with us on our train.

I hovered in the farthest corner of my bed as they approached. They were so-o-o-o tall that they walked right up to my top bunk and still had room to spare to be able to look at me and talk to me. But I was too scared to listen or respond, and I was glad when they finally, although smiling, turned away to talk to other families. Soon thereafter, we were told to get ready to leave. So we bundled up, grabbed our belongings, and headed into the cold to join all the other refugee families gathered in front of the building.

Several horse-drawn flatbed wagons appeared, and the military personnel directed us to get on, after supplying us with a number of woolen blankets to protect us during the ride through the storm ahead. For a fleeting moment, I remembered those refugee children I had seen back in Pulsnitz who were being transported on the exact same type of flatbed wagon without protection from the fierce winter conditions. And now we were no longer onlookers, but it was actually happening to us too. Apparently, the Bavarian government had instructed each farmer in the vicinity to take in one refugee family (*Flüchtlinge*), and that was where they were taking us.

It was extremely cold; it was snowing and the wind was howling, the infamous winter of 1945. We were at least six families, mothers with their kids, who huddled under the blankets that had been handed to us. The Gellners were not among us, as they had earlier gotten off the train at another station. I have no information on how they fared. All I know is that eventually they wound up back in East Germany by choice.

The horses pulled us slowly through the snow-blown country landscape, fighting against the whirling snow and gusting wind, stopping at one farmhouse after the other to drop off one family at a time. It may sound romantic, but I assure you, it was not. No one was smiling. We were delivered to a small farm in a village called Hundham, southeast of Neumarkt St. Veit. It was from Hundham that my mother sent her remaining postcards to my father's field number, one day apart. The significance of these postcards will be revealed as this story unfolds.

The farmers were not particularly thrilled to have us. They resented the fact that we were forced onto them. We were the *Flüchtlinge* (refugees), the uninvited "damned Prussians" coming from the north. We lived in one of the upstairs rooms. Our room held two beds, again with straw mattresses, a small table, and a small stove. My mother slept with one of her children, and the other bed was shared by the two remaining children. I don't recall who did what. My baby sister slept in the carriage. Adjoining this room was a very tiny chamber. My mother stored the black trunk and whatever few belongings we owned in this small storage space.

My mother told me of a rather comical but touching moment when she was unpacking and organizing our few belongings once we arrived at our room at the farm in Hundham. My brother Tom, who was four years old, observing her activities, suddenly rushed over to my mother and excitedly asked, "Mutti, Mutti, did you bring your softies with you?" She looked down at him and was puzzled. As he continued talking, he reached up to feel my mother's breasts, then took a deep sigh of relief and said, "*Gott sei Dank* (thank God), you brought them with you!" Honest and innocent as only a child can be. Such were the priorities of a young child in a world in turmoil.

I have a few words about those straw mattresses. Have you ever slept on one? If not, don't bother to find out. They are the most uncomfortable, irritating piece of home equipment one can imagine. The straw pieces pierced through the cover and scratched your body while you slept. Also, there were bedbugs that bit you. As much as we fought on the train to be allowed to sleep on such a mattress, this luxury had worn thin, and we realized that these mattresses were anything but comfortable. I guess the privilege of lying down versus sitting up on the train compensated for the utmost discomfort of such a prickly straw mattress at that time.

The days and weeks that finally brought us out of this dreadful winter and into spring were only an improvement in the weather, but not at all a safer existence for any of us. The early months of 1945 in Bavaria were absolute chaos. In this part of the country, it was not the Russians but the Americans who were still actively engaged in the war against us, the Germans, and at times it was ugly. I guess there was a sense in the air that the end was near. The German units were in disarray, and there were people of all sorts of nationalities wandering about aimlessly just trying to stay alive. Some were refugees from neighboring Slavic countries, and some were perhaps even defectors. No one asked any questions.

My mother was very cautious. She had some encounters with rather shady individuals who didn't speak German, and each time she cleverly steered out of their way when she suspected ill will on their parts. One of those individuals constantly stared at me while trying to distract my mother during a train ride to Neumarkt St. Veit. My mom was on to him. At the next stop, just before the train started again, she quickly opened the door, grabbed me, and jumped out. She fooled him, and he didn't make it out in time to pursue us. As she looked back, she saw him standing at the train door; he had jumped up from his seat as well, and now his eyes followed our escape. She had been right to suspect him.

It was during the time we lived in Hundham that I actually saw, not just heard, the planes and witnessed the dropping of bombs. No one who has heard the high-pitch whistle a bomb makes as it leaves the plane will ever forget it. Watching the bombs drop to earth is scary enough, but what is even more chilling is the short span of silence just before they hit with shattering impact. I, of course, did not know that the silence of the bombs before impact was caused by the sound delay in relation to the distance from me. This scene was played out before my eyes almost daily.

I didn't really know what the planes were aiming at. Little did I know that Munich and its surrounding areas had been the target of the American bombers since 1940, and the war was still raging. Where we were, there was only farmland, small towns and villages as far as I was concerned, but it made no difference to the attackers. More realistically, the Allies were still destroying railroad tracks and bridges and picked targets at random without cause or sense. Some of those bomb droppings were rather close by. I remember following the adults out to the fields and looking in total amazement at a large crater that had torn up a field just the day before. We saw more of those craters later on; some of them still had the bomb partially sticking out from the center, which seemed to make the grown-ups rather nervous as they hurried us away from the site. The countryside was littered with bomb craters.

Just weeks before the end of the war in 1945, when German defenses were almost non-existant, the furious bombings that had destroyed so many cities escalated needlessly. Small towns and villages of little or no military significance which were previously spared became helpless targets. People just walking and farmers doing their chores seemed to be intentionally struck down from the air. On March 19, scenic Muehldorf am Inn, perhaps 10 miles from Hundham where we lived at the time, was unexpectedly hit, killing 130 civilians and their farm animals. [14] About two years later our family would move to Muehldorf. The bombed out buildings still stood and we children found it intriguing to climb around inside, being totally unaware of the imminent danger of further collapse or our possible slipping during our escapades.

No wonder when I saw some episodes of *Twelve O'clock High* later as an adult in America, it left me with physical unease. There were the American pilots finding a target below and victoriously releasing a stream of bombs and then, satisfied, giving each other a thumbs-up before banking their planes towards their home base. As those bombs whistled towards earth, all I could think was, *Wait a minute—there are people down there!* Only one who has been *down there* would think and feel that way.

War is dirty, no matter which side of the fence you are on. In the end, no one comes out with clean hands. It is my deepest wish that the powers involved have learned a lesson. A notable quotation says it all: "Those who cannot remember the past are condemned to repeat it," as stated by Spanish-born American poet and philosopher George Santayana.

As described above, the years immediately following capitulation subjected the German population to continued hardship and despair in form of homelessness, starvation and disease. The caloric contents of the national rations were less than adequate and many succumbed and died. The homeless - there were many - and the orphaned children roamed the streets begging for food. Some of the hungry and desperate resorted to eating grass, I was told. Both Tante Ali (Berlin) and Tante Lis (Dresden) mentioned that people were in such distress and despair that suicide was the way out for a great number of them.[15] [16]

Each family was allotted food stamps, which were distributed in the nearby town of Neumarkt St. Veit. With these, my mother could obtain specific staple food items or sometimes clothing for us children, perhaps socks and shoes. And so, on a number of occasions, my mother and the four of us set out to reach that town on foot.

At first we walked on the open road, my mother pushing my sister's baby carriage and followed by her other three children. It was a long walk, but it was a necessary one, and remember, my mother needed her children by her side at all times. The thought of leaving us behind did not even enter her mind. Later my mother had to change her approach and walk through the thick forest. She had a difficult choice to make: walk through the forest and possibly encounter an attack by foot soldiers or one of those stray foreigners, or walk out in the open and be spotted by the American planes from above and fall victim to their random strafing attacks.

I can recall one such incident very clearly. We were walking to town, out in the open. It was a sunny day with blue skies, actually a delightful spring day. Suddenly we heard that familiar humming of multiple plane engines. We all looked up and searched the skies. At first we could not see anything, but then we spotted them, like silver fish in the air, rather small, flying in formation. They came closer and became larger, and suddenly one after the other broke the formation and dove earthward! They were strafing, shooting at anything that moved below. Since there was only farmland all around us, I suspect that they were aiming at people in the fields. Quite possibly they may even have spotted us! My mother was not going to second-guess their intent.

My mother took each one of us and flung us into the ditch nearby and commanded us not to move. Then she followed with my sister in her arms, and we stayed there for quite some time, it seemed, until the danger was over. It was especially difficult for us to remain still because my mother had thrown us directly into a bed of nettle plants (*Brennessel*). These plants somewhat resemble poison ivy, but with a different effect on your skin. When their sharp spiny leaf ends touch your skin, you immediately receive rather severe burning stings, not just one but several, and you show instant welts all over. The good thing is, the welts go away after a few hours, and that is that. They do not linger, itch, and ooze like poison ivy—thank God!

Would you believe that on one of those trips to obtain the family's food stamps, which included tobacco, it was loudly declared by a spokes*man*, "And for women, there won't be no smoker cards—not never" (using double and triple negatives, true translation of Bavarian dialect *nimmer net*). My mother was so insulted and upset; after all, she was a smoker! Talk about discrimination. But those were the new rules: women were no longer allowed to smoke.

After her experience with the American planes in open land, my mother decided to take the chance and walk through the dangerous forest. Later she told me that she was holding her breath the entire time and was looking all around us for possible suspicious characters who could do us harm. She was always relieved to see a sign of civilization on the other end of the dark forest. We heard the planes above us, but we knew they could not see us. We would have been free game; it was the bitter end of a brutal, senseless war. We children, on the other hand, innocently looked forward to the other side of the forest only because there stood a house that had a swinging bench in the yard that we were allowed to sit on. What a delightful treat!

One bright and sunny day, my mother and I were outside the farmhouse. She was washing laundry by hand, using a scrub board, and I was helping her hang some of the easier pieces. All of a sudden and out of nowhere, an American plane (did I see a white star on the side of the plane?) came towards us and dipped right down towards the farmhouse. It came so low and so close that I could see the pilot. My mother grabbed my hand, and we ran inside the house. He didn't do anything; he just swooped down really close and climbed right up again. I don't think he was on a sightseeing mission, and as I realize now, he had no ill will and thus we were spared. At least, I would like to think that. But what if we had been men?

Those trips to town I mentioned earlier were absolutely necessary to redeem the food and clothing stamps for their indicated value. I remember our first pair of wooden shoes— yes, *wooden* shoes. We were thrilled! They were handmade from wooden blocks with leather straps. The hinge that enabled you to walk was also made of leather; however, we found out very quickly that more often than not, the two individual wooden pieces pinched your foot. We learned to step very carefully, and running was out of the question. Barefoot was still the way to go for us kids. But having wooden shoes certainly came in handy in some instances. It definitely beat walking barefoot across a field of cut wheat and having the stubby dry stalks pierce the soles of your feet or stepping onto a cow pie and having that smelly substance squeeze between your toes! Yuck.

We were always hungry, and it was especially difficult for us kids to see the abundance of food the farmers had and to watch the farmer's kids as well as the farmhands satisfy their appetites in front of us as they sat around the main table each day after they returned from working in the fields. There was always a bowl of fresh cow's milk in the middle of the table into which the farmers and farmhands dipped their pieces of that oh-so-scrumptious farmer's bread. The milk showed a buttery layer on the surface, and the bread had this heavenly aroma, both of which are hard to forget. We were just drooling and swallowing in imaginary participation as we watched. They knew we were standing there, and on more than one occasion, they told us to go away.

Once in a while, though, my mother got some food items from the farm, probably in secret from one of the farmhands who had befriended her. My mother was indeed blessed with a guardian angel in the form of a live-in farmhand named Fanni. She liked my mother and realized quickly how hard it must have been for her to feed her four children. Fanni would often sneak food items to her, whatever was easy to smuggle upstairs. My mother created miracles with whatever she received. She got a calf's brain once, fried it and then spoon-fed it to each of us. I can still taste this delicacy—it was heavenly!

Every so often, we got some eggs and slices of bread, potatoes and maybe some bacon slabs for rendering into the most memorable, delicious spread my siblings and I still remember with joy. The bacon was cut into very small pieces, and perhaps a diced onion was added. Then it was carefully cooked in pork fat or lard until the bacon pieces became crisp and the onions turned yellow or very light brown. It was then poured into a heat-resistant bowl for hardening. This spread lasted for some time. Although we all ate it a lot, it never ceased being our favorite. It was most delicious on slices of farmer's bread sprinkled with salt—yum!

Still in Hundham, my mother was appalled as she watched the farmer's wife cutting long strips of smoked bacon and handing some of those strips to her little son to play with. Of course, he was just a kid and didn't know any better. His mother was the one who had little regard for our hard times and how hungry someone else could be. They resented us, the *Fluechtlinge*, so much so that they carried any surplus food to the local priest rather than give it to us, which would have been the Christian if not the humane thing to do. The local church had it pretty good in those days, as other farmers felt the same way and showered them with gifts. Do you suppose they hoped to barter their way into heaven? I wonder if they ever got there! Oh, this sounds rather bitter—sorry!

At a time of national rationing and overall starvation of the German people, my mother became very creative with preparing meals for us. We were luckier than city dwellers as we lived in the countryside where we could help ourselves to what nature had to offer. Mushroom and berry picking became a fun thing to do for the entire family. There were three different types of mushrooms we all learned about as being safe: (1) *Steinpilze*, which were round, brown, and had a somewhat slimy cap with a spongelike yellow underside; (2)*Pfifferlinge*, which were orange tulip trunks called chanterelle; and (3) *Champignons*, the little white mushrooms as we know them here in the U.S. The mushrooms were all wild, not artificially farmed. The berries we most frequently picked were blueberries, raspberries, blackberries, and wild strawberries (the little ones).

Cherries and other tree fruits were another story. Of course, here we had to ask the farmers. My brother Mike had befriended some older boys, sons of wealthy farmers in a village nearby. They had told him that he could come to their farm and they would give him bushels of cherries. He believed them and told Mutti about it. It sounded good, and she was touched by their generosity. So Mike and I set off one afternoon to get those cherries for the family.

The walk was long and difficult, as it was uphill for most of the way. We finally came to the crest and spotted the farm. When we arrived there, the entire family and all the farm-hands were sitting down for dinner. We stood near the door and realized how hungry we were. The people knew we were there but did not invite us to join them. We waited patiently until they said their prayers of thanks and started to disburse.

The boys whom Mike had befriended came out and wanted to know what we were doing there. Mike told them the reason, and suddenly they all started to laugh out loud, bending over and gesturing at us. One of them said something very strange: "Da lach ich mir ja ein Loch in den Bauch" (I'm going to laugh a hole into my belly). I was trying to envision this strange phenomenon. As I was still in my puzzled state, the boys began shoving Mike around, and we both decided to make a run for it. After a while, when it was safe, we slowed down. We walked more and more slowly as we tried to figure out how to go home without the fruit. Mutti was going to be so disappointed. But all I remember is that Mutti just put her arms around us quietly and then proceeded to make us scrambled eggs with chives.

They were the best eggs we ever had. Our guardian angel, Fanni, had just handed my mother the eggs – bless her.

Mike and I were old enough to go to school. Mike was nine, and I had turned six in April 1945. Since everything had been destroyed, even in the countryside, we attended school in a small one-room house: grades 1–4 in the morning, the next four grades in the afternoon. Who could learn anything under these circumstances? But these were the rules.

Here I must describe something that seems rather gross to me just thinking back—lice! We all had them. No matter how diligently my mother tried to comb them out with a special fine-toothed comb, it was of no use. In class they would just jump onto you from the neighboring kid and yours back to them. We did a lot of scratching until scabs formed quickly. We all had eczema with large scabby blotches all over our bodies. I still show the scars from them, especially on my legs. How did we get rid of these disgusting afflictions? Read on . . .

And then came the Americans! One day in May 1945, without warning, we heard a roar that came closer and closer. Sometimes the roar was mixed with a screeching sound like rusty wheels or chains. What was it? My mother was not happy. She sensed something was about to happen, but we could not see anything yet.

And then they came around the neighboring farm-house—the American tanks, one after the other. One of them turned alongside the broad side of our farmhouse, and as they drove up, to my astonishment, I saw a soldier peeking out the top of the tank level with our window—and we were on the second floor! My mother quickly hid her valuables, like the camera and her jewelry, in the baby carriage. Her diamond ring wound up in my sister's dry baby formula.

Then the soldiers came into the farmhouse, and after a short pause at the farmer's residence downstairs, we heard their footsteps coming up the stairs. Because my mother was so apprehensive, so were we children. Then the door opened, and two American MPs stood there in full, imposing uniform. They were so tall that they had to stoop down to fit under the door frame to enter our room.

Much to their surprise, my mother began speaking in flawless English and explained who we were and that we had nothing for them. The MPs smiled politely, probably because they were surprised to hear someone speak their language, and backed out of our room the way they had come in. You see, in those days, very few people in Germany spoke English unless they had been educated overseas or had a background like my parents where the English language had been used fluently. My mother's mother being from Wales, my mother herself having been born in China thus making her first spoken language English, and my father having worked for Shell Oil in London for many years as a young man provided all the background the Bierlings needed to be fluent in English.

There was another tense situation shortly thereafter when my mother heard the farm dog barking angrily. Not wanting my little sister to wake up from her nap, she stepped onto the balcony to see what was going on. I was right behind her. We noticed an American on a motorcycle driving at high speed around the manure pile in the middle of the farm courtyard, followed by the angry dog. Then, to my mother's horror, the soldier pulled out his service revolver and was about to shoot the dog. She didn't think twice and abandoned the possibility of being shot herself. Without hesitation she let the soldier have it in perfect English and with such fury that he looked up at her in surprise, smiled sheepishly, put the gun back into the holster, and drove away. The dog would live! This was the second time I heard my mother use these strange-sounding words to communicate, but apparently, whatever words her lecture contained had their aimed effect.

The American troops made various farmhouses their headquarters. Our farm was too small to house even a small group of soldiers. We children visited those at the neighboring farms. One time we proudly came home with our very first chocolate bar, which one of the soldiers had given us. My mother inspected it and then approved it for consumption.

Actually, we were lucky that we encountered rather friendly and compassionate Americans then. What we did not know was that we Germans were not well regarded or, should I say, even hated. As I found out later growing up, we were the enemy, and the leaders of our country had caused the war that cost so many lives on all sides.

The dislike or hatred of the Germans came especially alive with the discovery of the atrocities at the concentration camps, some of which were liberated by Allied troops. On April 11, 1945, Buchenwald was liberated by the Sixth Armored Division of General Patton's Third Army, and on April 29, 1945, Dachau was liberated by the U.S. Seventh Army. What they found there understandably repulsed and infuriated the military men, and news spread quickly. While GIs were not nearly as brutal as were the Soviets in their advance across Poland and eastern Germany, the first discoveries of the concentration camps resulted in a heavy-handed approach by American troops towards Germans, civilians and soldiers alike. April 1945 was a month filled with some of the most brutal fighting of the war, as the horrors of the Nazi regime were revealed to the world. Thank God our little village of Hundham deep in the Bavarian countryside northeast of Munich placed us somewhat on the sidelines of the above-mentioned last weeks of desperate and fierce fighting, but it was by no means safe.

From the air, as the Americans sat in their fighter planes, the individual German was not a personal entity, just a group as a whole that needed to be destroyed. Later the military units on the ground met the German population face-to-face, and as far as we noticed, their attitude in many cases was quite different and more humane, especially towards the "little people," us children.

In general, the German people were still leery of the Americans. Throughout the preceding years and intensifying during 1944 and the early months of 1945, they were menacing us from the air; and sometime in May 1945 (I assume after capitulation on May 8), they were on the ground. Viewed through the eyes of a child, they were real people like us; yet in our observation, they were also different in many ways: the uniform they wore, the language they spoke, their unfamiliar mannerisms, their gum chewing, the relaxed and friendly way they communicated with one another, and, quite surprisingly, their fondness for children. In my recollection, we were more afraid of German uniformed men with their stern and authoritative demeanor than we were of the Americans. How strange is that?

The American occupation in our village did not last long before they had to move on. But before they did, I must tell you, they made sure that they purified our water and that all of us were clean of bugs and disease. They lined us all up and sprayed us with DDT, and that took care of it. Much later we learned this white powder, DDT, was not really such a wonder drug and in some cases rather detrimental. As far as I know, none of us had an adverse reaction to this treatment—and the lice were gone!

Our positive impression of the Americans was perhaps the result of my mother's English language skills with which she was able to communicate with them, often triggering surprise then understanding smiles and adoring glances at her children. Quite frankly, the Americans' smiles were the first smiles I had seen in a long time. Up until then, for most of my young years, life had been a serious matter and nothing to smile about.

The Americans showered us with candy and chocolate, items that we had not seen since before our flight from home in February 1945. The labels were in a different language, but that made no difference to us, as we didn't know how to read anyway. Besides, a hungry child does not scrutinize covers or labels; that was my mother's job.

I have heard of incidents of rape and other criminal acts committed by the occupying Americans, but as small as I was, I do not recall one moment when my mother was in such distress or had to compromise her existence as a female and as our mother. My mother was a lady with unquestionable stature, but she also let it be known that she had no reluctance to fiercely protect her family. It must have left an impression and as a result she was treated with respect, and our encounters with the Americans came and went without disturbance or threat at any time.

7

POW Camp Bad Aibling

And where was my father all this time? Apparently, his unit was in the Ukraine when my father was injured as a shell exploded near him. He and a number of others in his battalion were shipped back to Germany for treatment. After recuperation, they were heading back to join their unit and were subsequently captured by the Americans. My father thus became a prisoner of war with the United States Army and along with thousands of others was placed in the prison camp at the airport outside of Bad Aibling in southern Bavaria. His original unit apparently was shipped out to Siberia, and none of them were ever seen again. The war would officially rage in Germany until early May of that year.

The top brass of the American military running the prison camp in Bad Aibling, Bavaria, needed to communicate with the prisoners and requested an interpreter. Out of the crowd of thousands cowering in the field, my father, who could speak English, raised his hand, and so he became the official interpreter. He befriended the major for whom he worked, and one day while they were chatting, the major wanted to know whether my father had a family. He replied, yes, he did—a wife and four kids. Did my father know where his family was? This was not a strange question at all, as in those days, with all the destruction and confusion and families being torn apart, no one knew where anybody was. But my father said, yes, he knew precisely. You see, the only postcard my father had received from my mother was also the very last one she had sent from our last position in Hundham. Doesn't that give you goose bumps?

The major thought for an instant and then surprised my father with, "Fred, start walking." I guess he was quite taken by the fact that in the tumultuous disarray that now ruled over Germany, here was *one* family who had a chance to reunite. He handed my father his official release papers and bid him farewell. The date of his release was June 11, 1945, five days before my father's forty-second birthday. I later found these discharge papers in my father's records. The name of this wonderful man who authorized my father's release was Major H. J. Rolin, CAC Executive, 214th Antiaircraft Artillery Gun BN, APO 758, U.S. Army at Bad Aibling Prisoner of War Camp, Bad Aibling Airport, Germany. I have often regretted that I did not seek out the family of this kind man to express our gratitude and thanks. There must have been a special connection that the major and my father developed over the weeks and months they worked together—the captor and the captive, a most unlikely duo.

My father was extremely lucky. German POWs in the many camps throughout Germany lived outdoors in fields surrounded by barbed-wire fence while being guarded at gunpoint by the Americans. A friend of mine recalled that when he stayed at Bad Aibling POW camp, he witnessed women from town tossing food across the fence to the starving prisoners. The well-meaning women were promptly shot at by the Americans, wounding a number of them. Reports have it that hundreds of thousands died of starvation, exposure or untreated illnesses in the months which followed capitulation.[17]

My father never spoke to us about his personal experiences and his corresponding emotions at that camp before his assignment as interpreter—not ever. In fact, he never spoke about any part of his military assignments or actions. He had committed those into the deepest chambers of his memory to remain untold.

Although Germany had capitulated on May 8, the hostilities in other places in the world, such as the Pacific war theater, continued to rage until the end of September 1945. On August 6, 1945, the U.S. dropped the first atomic bomb on Hiroshima and three days later another one on Nagasaki. The Japanese surrender came on August 14, 1945.

My father had always been a fantastic communicator and diplomat and an upright individual with enormous scruples. This honesty and righteousness he then passed on to us as we started out in life, and we have since dutifully lived our lives according to those principles. As you will read later on, he continued to be a liaison and public relations advocate between the German and American governments in the postwar years that followed his release.

After receiving his release papers, my father immediately set out on foot to reach his family close to a hundred kilometers away. It was still a dangerous undertaking for him back in June 1945, walking alone through the countryside. Word about the capitulation in Germany was slow to penetrate the population, and there was tremendous uncertainty and mistrust. There was the unsettling presence of strange individuals, some in dilapidated uniforms who were perhaps deserters and others who were homeless refugees from eastern European countries, all appearing out of nowhere, wandering about and looking for food and shelter or for a hiding place. It was definitely not safe, and my father risked being caught again—or worse. His release papers would help to clear his name but were certainly no free pass to safety in unstable surroundings. I understand that at one point my father came upon the Red Cross (Rote Kreuz), and with their help, he was able to find Hundham and ultimately his family.

Tom, Sabine, and I visited this site in May 2009 and found the abandoned army base completely unchanged, empty and dismissed. It was a ghost town, yet still telling the stories of its history, and that touched us deeply. After all, it represented an important part of our family through our father.

Finding the former POW camp site in Bad Aibling was not an easy task. It was similar to the time when Tom and I searched for our intended destination in Dresden in 1994. Again, we had no idea what exactly we were looking for. All we knew, the camp was at or near the former airport. The townspeople were not particularly helpful and sent us in conflicting directions. Exhausted and disappointed we finally followed a road that lead out of town and unexpectedly while halting at a stop sign, we came face-to-face with two stone pillars that seemed to 'call out' to us to drive through and investigate what lied beyond. It did not take us long to realize that we had indeed found the POW camp. Isn't it astounding that we seemed to have a guiding hand so often in our lives! – how humbling and reassuring.

One of the buildings displayed a large clock that had lost its pointers and blankly stared back at us. We saw the fields where the prisoners had been held, surrounded by tall fences. The fences were still there, but the barbed wire was gone. We saw the main building displaying English language signs from its days of American occupation. The large entrance hall of the headquarters building had a lonely chandelier hanging above an empty floor. The former housing quarters for military families at that base stood seemingly abandoned only yesterday, but the rotting wooden balconies told the real story of time elapsed.

We were very moved as we walked around the grounds and imagined moments and events past. We did notice though that there was ongoing construction of apartment buildings on the base, indicating that eventually the grounds would be occupied and the property re-landscaped.

Not much was spoken between us as we set out to continue our trip toWasserburg and on to Muehldorf. Our forlorn thoughts were rapidly brought back to reality when we encountered a traffic jam caused by a motor cycle accident many kilometers up ahead. When at last we settled in our hotel room in Muehldorf were we able to recall the events of the day and discuss our emotions about it.

A bit of history: The former POW camp where my father was held was taken over by the U.S. Army in 1952 and was converted by the United States Army Security Agency (ASA) to a communications monitoring station for American intelligence. In 1971 the National Security Agency (NSA) and the U.S.Department of Defense took over command from the U.S. Army. In 1994, the NSA transferred command of its Bad Aibling base to INSCOM, one of the Central Security Services of USA.

Bad Aibling Station was closed on September 30, 2004. The base was then returned to the Federal Republic of Germany.[18]

8

Reunion and Our Journey Onward

Now back to spring of 1945 before my father's release from POW camp: As you will recall, my mother had befriended a young farmhand named Fanni. One day Fanni offered to read my mother's palm. My mother replied, "Nonsense, I don't believe in that." But Fanni insisted—just for fun, she said. Looking at my mother's palm, she told her, "Your husband will come home. He will come home on a Friday, and I will see him first." That sounded too good to be true, and my mother smiled.

We children noticed that when my mother did her housework, whether it was washing dishes, preparing meals, or hand washing laundry, she would always face out one particular window in the room. This gave her an overview of a road that wound its way up a hill and then disappeared around the corner of the next farmhouse. One day my brother Tom and I were playing in a puddle of rainwater when suddenly my mother came charging out of the house, ripping off her apron and running up the hill. Our eyes followed her direction, and we saw a soldier walking towards us, having just come around that very corner my mother had been observing relentlessly all these months.

My mother ran as fast as she could and then flung her arms around him, and the two stood there for quite some time. They were too far away for us to recognize that the soldier was actually our father. And here comes the shocker: Fanni was right. My father *did* come home on a Friday, and she *did* see him first. You see, she was working the hay fields up on the hillside when she spotted a soldier walking down the road. She threw down her rake and rushed over to him and said to him while pointing, "You must be Fred. Your family lives down there in that farmhouse!" It's hard to believe, but it is the truth. Do you believe in miracles? I do.

Note: A few years later, my parents apparently went back to Hundham to find Fanni. They learned that she had married an undertaker, and her name was now Fanni Haberger. She lived in Neumarkt St. Veit, the town where my mother and we children were first dropped off from the train after our infamous flight. It was a tearful reunion.

We were a family again! My father soon found a job in the town of Muehldorf, at least ten miles from Hundham. On July 1, 1945, he was hired by the Landratsamt (local government offices) as an interpreter and liaison between the German and American military governments. Somehow my father got hold of an old rusty bicycle with which he was able to get to work every day. Many years later when I was an adult, I revisited Hundham, but by car. Driving down the road from Muehldorf via Moessling to Hundham, I realized what a miserable trip this must have been for my father on a rusty bike. There was one hill after the other. How did he do it?

Yet each day on his way home, my father would stop at the old mill to pick up bags of oats or ground wheat. He paid very little for it or sometimes got it for free, as the ground-up product was the scraps from around the millstones. But it was most important to him that the family was fed. Each morning before he set out on his bike to Muehldorf, he prepared *angebrannte Griess Suppe* (browned farina soup). He took a little fat—any scrap of fat, probably from the *hamster* cup—and browned the farina in it. He added lots of water and some salt, covered it and left for work. We all just loved this soup. We had it every day and yet did not tire of it.

To go begging, or *hamstern*, became an activity that Mike and I were called upon to do, since we were the two oldest children. Every day we set out with a little white metal cup with a blue rim and handle and went from farmhouse to farmhouse begging for food, sometimes walking great distances between the scattered villages. We would come home with a few slices of bread, an egg or two, and that little metal cup full or not so full of spoonfuls of various fats, lard, or even butter all placed together into that cup. The contents of this cup took on a mosaic of colors: yellow, white, gray—a concoction of various forms of fat for consumption. Yet my mother was thrilled with everything.

Hamstern was not always a rewarding experience. Some of the farmers slammed the door in our faces. Maybe Mike's outlandish lines at times were the cause for that. Mike had a witty mind and a mouthpiece to go with it. When things got really annoying or hopeless, he would retaliate with his warped sense of humor, which was not always appreciated.

An afterthought to our straw mattresses: Soon after their reunion, my parents made a ceremonious trip to the outskirts of town to dump the contents of those mattresses and returned home victoriously. Sleeping was a lot more comfortable from then on, we all agreed. Whatever the new mattresses were filled with, it was *not* straw, and we didn't care what substance replaced it.

As the winter drew near, my father thought it best that we move closer to Muehldorf, as his bicycle was not going to do the trick over the winter months. And so we moved to

Moessling, about halfway to Muehldorf, to the largest farmhouse in the village. The owners of the farm in Moessling had two sons, Konrad and Alois, and at least three daughters, as I recall.

Forty years after we had moved away, I revisited this farm with my husband and we met the oldest son, Konrad, who had taken over the farm from his father, as is customary. Konrad's son, daughter-in-law, and grandson lived there as well. I met the young daughter-in-law, a somewhat shy little thing. Pregnant with her second child, she was obviously being trained to become the next mistress of this establishment.

My mother had always liked the younger Loisl (short for Alois) better than Konrad. Loisl had more charm and compassion and was always smiling and in good spirits. According to my mother, he would have made a much better farm master than his older brother. Konrad seemed to be more on the harsh and cold side and wasn't quite as sociable, if at all. Yet when I met Konrad in 1987, once he figured out that I was Elsie's oldest daughter of so many years ago, he broke into tears. We hugged one another and stood so for a long moment, both crying. Since my husband did not speak German and had no idea what was going on, he was left with awkwardly standing on the sideline and simply observing this heartwarming scene of recognition and welcome. After inquiring about Loisl, I was told that he had married a girl in the next village and still operated his own farm there.

Our nostalgic return to Moessling in 2009, another twenty-two years after my above-mentioned visit, was again a touching, heartwarming encounter with the Niederschweiberer family and will live in our memories forever. This time, Tom, Sabine and I met the young offspring of Konrad's son and his wife, who are now running the farm. We met the charming young lady, Marlene, who was the expected second child of twenty-two years earlier. They are a lovely family, and all are involved in one chore or another around the farm. Marlene's brother, although younger, is presently being groomed to be the next farm master. And so it goes, generation after generation. We were amazed that Konrad and his wife were still alive to give us a hearty welcome with smiles and hugs. Konrad is now eighty-four years old.

Once again, back to 1946–47: The farm in Moessling definitely had more food available, and sometimes we were the beneficiaries of items like smoked sausage after a slaughter or a pigeon that had gotten caught in the wheels of the sliding gates to the farm that were closed each evening. One little pigeon went a long way among six hungry mouths, with my mother the miracle worker in charge!

We kids were always hungry, though, and so we readily volunteered to work in the potato fields during harvest so we could sneak a raw potato every so often. Raw potatoes were a delicacy as far as we were concerned, not only in the field, dirt and all, but also at home. Whenever my mother peeled potatoes, we gathered around her so she could give us a piece or maybe two of a raw potato.

Many times my mother was given some pork lard and strips of bacon. Gloriously she would come upstairs to our living quarters and proceed to render the lard and fry the cubed bacon with diced onion in it. This mixture was then stored in our food chamber, a small crawl space in a cool, unheated location where we kept our food. Refrigeration was an unthought-of luxury then. And yes, we still had our browned farina soup every morning.

The farmer also had a food chamber, a very small storage room specifically designated for food items. Every day the cook would carry the uneaten *Dampfnudeln* (a flat yeast dough steamed in milk and butter) into that chamber to be cut up for the pigs the next day. We kids knew where the chamber was, and Mike—who else—would climb through the window and hand us the cold *Dampfnudeln*, which were about the size of an adult hand. Then we would all run off to a nearby secluded hiding place to feast on them. In God's eyes, were we thieves?

What you must know is that the daily routine of preparing the food for the evening meal was one of the most important tasks the cook had to perform before going out to give a helping hand in the fields. Each morning she would prepare the yeast dough for the Dampfnudeln, form the individual balls and place them covered on a large board to rise while she was gone. Well, here comes my little brother, Tom, finds the covered board and proceeds to reshape the balls into rings, pretzels and whatever shape he could think of! He carefully replaced the covering cloth and placed the board back in its original location. You can imagine the turmoil which could be heard from the kitchen when the cook returned in the afternoon to prepare the evening meal for the rest of the farm crew.

The hay barn was a fun place for us kids. Guess who discovered that we could climb to the top of the piled up hay inside the loft, sit on a bale, and drop down to the bottom, which, thank heavens, was padded with loose hay to absorb our impact? Yes, Mike. And again, the farmer spoiled it for us. He just did not have any understanding of what kids consider fun. Grown-ups!

Do you perhaps get the notion that Mike was quite a character and full of mischief? You are right. One day he and some of his friends set out to raid the bee house on the farm next door. Of course, I was in tow—the only girl. Mike knew exactly where to go, how to find the smoker pipe, and then how to light it and puff it near the hives long enough to permit us to lift out the honeycombs. We quickly went to an old abandoned car and proceeded to munch on that sweet delight.

Suddenly we heard the beekeeper's yelling as he came running towards us wielding a pitchfork. The boys quickly climbed a rather high slatted wooden fence and disappeared. I was not as swift in fence climbing and got stuck on the barbed wire that ran across the top. Mike turned around when he heard my screams and pulled the wire out of my thigh and helped me over to the other side. The scars on my leg are still there to remind me.

Yes, Mike was a troublemaker that the farmers did not always appreciate. You see, Mike had learned to imitate the rooster, so every evening until the farmer figured out what was happening, Mike would stick his head deep into the chicken coop and "rooster" until all the hens sounded out in excited chicken chatter and the entire coop was in an uproar. They definitely had no interest in laying eggs then, and the farmer was not happy. I wonder what Mike was telling them. The farmer certainly did not wonder or care—there was trouble! My mother was told in no uncertain terms that she better rein in her son—or else.

My little sister, in the meantime, had become a cute little toddler. Her fun consisted of playing with little chicks or kittens behind the barn.

There were certain festivities on the farm that meant there was the possibility of special food items coming our way. For instance, Easter Sunday was one. I recall one of the farmer's daughters, probably with the permission of her father, promising to let us sit at the head table for Easter dinner if we would go to church with them. We eagerly agreed.

So Easter Sunday came around, and we were excited to fulfill our promise to go to church. Mutti silently prepared our skimpy wardrobe by using the farmer's iron. It was not electric, so one needed to place hot coals into it to create the required heat. We then went to the Catholic church with the farmer's family. I do remember how utterly cold the church was and how inappropriately dressed we were. But we had no other clothes, and well, at least they were ironed.

Everything done and spoken was very new and bewildering to us. I also thought it was strange when one of the farmer's girls took a chain of rosary beads and wove them between my fingers in a certain way that only she and the other parishioners were familiar with. I let her weave the beads into my fingers, and I followed her every step—stand, sit, kneel, stand, kneel— wishing that it would all be over soon and I would be allowed to get some of their food to eat. Oh, it was so cold in that church! They kept their promise and invited us kids to the table. And yes, we were finally allowed to dip our bread pieces into that delicious bowl of milk with the rest of the dining family. Heavenly!

I do not recall my mother being part of this, not in church and not at the table. Later I found out why. While we were still in Hundham, before my father came home from the war, my mother received a visit from a Catholic priest who had walked quite a distance to find her. She was at first delighted to think that finally someone had compassion enough to give her some assistance. But she quickly learned that was not the case at all. In reality, his sole purpose for seeking out my mother was to tell her that since she, a Catholic, had married a Protestant man and had four children technically out of wedlock, she was living in sin and the Catholic Church had decided to excommunicate her.

My mother was briefly perplexed and gasped in disbelief, realizing the absurdity of this moment. With angry determination and utter disappointment in humanity, especially since it was ill displayed by a clergyman, she ordered him out of the house. In defiance, her will to survive grew even more intense. I believe that my mother's polite decline to the farmer's offer in Moessling to go to Mass and then join their Easter meal was probably exactly for that reason. My mother was a proud woman and certainly no hypocrite.

But she let her children go if it meant they got something decent to eat.

My mother remained steadfast in her resolution made in Hundham after the unfortunate incident with the priest. When the time came to choose our religious education, it was an easy decision: we were raised Lutheran, my father's faith, and attended a Lutheran church wherever we lived and received formal confirmation at age fourteen.

There were other memorable occasions on the farm in Moessling, such as the harvest celebration. Since we were always hungry, it is only natural that I would remember food items such as the delicious deep-fried doughnuts without jelly. Jelly doughnuts were only customary in the northern part of Germany, such as the city of Berlin, thus called Berliner Pfannkuchen, or in short 'Berliner'.[19] I also remember the flat fried dough called *Kücherl*, meaning "little cakes"; and the syrup that was extracted by boiling sugar beets. And then there was the slaughter of a cow and pigs. This remains a gruesome memory, as we had to listen to the screams of the pigs until they were silent. Mercifully, we did not see the means by which this was accomplished. At a later point, we were allowed to see the results of the slaughter. The dead carcass hung suspended by chains in one of the barns, and the farmers proceeded to cut off the meat to be smoked or to be turned into the most delicious sausages. Chickens were unique to watch. They were chased and then decapitated and, to our amazement, kept on running!

The fun part about those chains from which the slaughtered farm animals hung came afterwards when the chains were cleaned and converted into swings for us kids by placing a long wooden board onto the two hanging chain loops. Under supervision, we were allowed to sit on the board and swing back and forth while we let out excited shouts and squeals of delight. This lasted for only a few days, though, because the barn needed to be returned to its original useful state. But we enjoyed it while it lasted.

Our time in Moessling was the time immediately after the end of the war. It was in Moessling where Mike, Tom, and I found various military gear, from helmets and mess kits to rifles, hand grenades, and gas masks that had been discarded in the hills and fields by fleeing German Wehrmacht units. Mike tended the farmer's sheep, and Tom and I often made our way to him to keep him company. It was on those excursions when we located these discarded weapons. Thank God, we did not handle the hand grenades, although other kids did and got blown up as they proceeded to examine them. This paraphernalia was strewn all over the place. We did play with the gas masks, though. They had a strange rubbery smell and looked very scary once we put them on. We liked to frighten each other and laughed at the sounds we made talking through these masks.

Mike and I went to school in the next village. The classes were taught by female teachers, as there were no male teachers around. They had all been called to war, like it or not, just as my father had been, and had not yet returned or had been killed. The female teachers were quite mean to us, and we were very frightened of them. The use of thin springy whipping sticks was a daily occurrence for the slightest little thing you did or did not do.

It was a very cold winter morning when Mike and I walked to school through a driving snowstorm one day. We did not have adequate clothing or gloves. It took us longer than usual just to make it halfway to the village where the school was located, so Mike decided to turn back. His reasoning was that it was better not to show up for school than to get there late and endure that whip across our cold fingertips for every minute we were late. If you pulled back your hand as you anticipated the pain, the number of hits was increased. Both of us had experienced this punishment before, and I did not need much convincing to agree with him to turn around. Mutti understood and wrote an excuse note for us to the teacher. She also went to the schoolhouse in person to complain, but with little effect.

Our family finally moved to Muehldorf in 1947. We lived at Stadtplatz 4, right next to the town's entrance tower, on the fourth floor. My father still worked for the Landratsamt Muehldorf until August 20, 1948, when he joined the Military Government Liaison and Security Office, Detachment E 282, Landkreis Muehldorf, U.S. Army. The office occupied a huge building on the hill above town, and this structure may once have been a mansion or former official parliament building.

Part of the grounds clearly included the former greens or parks that had been converted into individual allotment gardens. As an employee of the American government, my father was given such garden space to work as he pleased. The family went up the town hill to our little garden quite often, and we children proudly helped plant and harvest the various vegetables for the family table. Secretly, though, it was more fun for us kids to run inside the furrows and try not to step on the vegetables while our parents gave us watchful glances.

Then the makeup of our private garden started to change. My parents, both smokers, began to plant tobacco to satisfy their habit. Though cigarettes were available on the black market or with stamps, my parents quickly used up their stamp allowance, since they had only my father's allotment to work with. The people who had cigarettes in abundance were the Americans, and my parents had already traded away priceless possessions, like the diamond ring my mother had hidden in my sister's formula and an expensive camera, in exchange for cigarettes. We were now harvesting tobacco.

My parents were now engaged in making their own cigarettes. We children witnessed their bringing home the big tobacco leaves, briefly steaming them or soaking them in boiling water (I am not sure which), and then hanging them up to dry in closets or in the city tower loft. They then cut the dried leaves into thin strips. The aroma, or smell to us kids, was not particularly pleasant.

I am not sure what paper my parents were able to use to roll these thin tobacco slivers into cigarettes and how long this cigarette home production lasted, but to my recollection, it passed quickly. Sadly, years later, the effects of cigarette smoking became a real health problem for both my parents.

A short time after we moved to Muehldorf, an old family friend from our home in Pulsnitz, Walter Faust, unexpectedly showed up at our doorstep. What I suspect is that he too had been enlisted in the German military and wound up in Bavaria at the end of the war. His wife, "Tante" Hanni (Hannelore Faust), was trapped back in Pulsnitz, which by then had become part of East Germany under the Communist regime. Tante Hanni was also the one who had been an eye-witness from her window just a block away of the horrifying burning of our home and the shooting of its inhabitants. Mutti apparently had notified her of our whereabouts once we settled in Bavaria and in return had received the ugly report of the demise of our home from her.

"Onkel" Walter stayed with us while Tante Hanni desperately tried to escape from East Germany to join him. She made several attempts in the dark of night to cross the border by walking through a thick forest. On one of those attempts, she was caught by the Russians, gang-raped by five of them and left for dead. She awoke alone in the forest, damaged physically and psychologically, and eventually stumbled back home. After she recovered, she gave it one more try and actually succeeded. She made her way south to Muehldorf, where she was reunited with her husband. Some time later they moved to Bad Duerkheim on the Mosel River, where Onkel Walter resumed his profession as a schoolteacher.

Tante Hanni, that sweet, frail little person, never had any children, as a result of the gang rape.

Starting in 1948, my father worked as an assistant at the Office of the United States High Commissioner for Germany, Office of Land Commissioner for Bavaria, until June 1950, where he worked as a liaison between the local government and the population of Muehldorf and villages in near proximity and the American military government. He had to attend many meetings and consult officials and political leaders.

I found a letter of commendation from the City of Muehldorf to my father, thanking him for his unrelenting work on behalf of the city with the American military government to achieve a substantial grant necessary to begin the rebuilding of this war-damaged town. How proud are we, his children, even sixty-one years later! Having gone on our nostalgic trip to Muehldorf in 2009 and seeing how this former medieval town had developed into a lovely, cosmopolitan showcase, we came away with the knowledge that our father had played a small but important role here.

It was also my father's commission to introduce the Americans and their way of life to the German public. He was given a jeep with a canvas top, as well as a projector and several movies on large spools, and he went on his way to the surrounding towns and villages to show off America to the ordinary Bavarian citizens. I was allowed to accompany him on several trips, and I was very proud of him as he stood there in front of the townspeople who came to listen. He always typically cleared his throat before beginning his presentation.

I saw on the townspeople's faces that they were absolutely fascinated by what was shown to them. My mouth must have stayed open several times during his show as well. For instance, we saw houses cut in half and transported down a highway, a rodeo, a Fourth of July picnic with all the traditions like pie eating and sack racing, a typical parade as well as a marching band during halftime at a football game, which in itself was unusual to watch—and then there were the skyscrapers of America's big cities! Certainly at that moment in time, neither my father nor the rest of our family had any idea that ten years later we ourselves would all live in the United States.

Since we lived on the top floor of the building next to the town tower of Muehldorf, my brother Mike showed us how to get inside the tower, and there he showed us the multitude of bats hanging upside down from the rafters during the day. In the early evenings, we looked out of our window and watched the bats' swooping flight patterns as they pursued their prey. So you see, we looked for and found our own entertainment, and in doing so, we learned quite naturally about the world around us.

Speaking of the windows on the fourth floor, my little sister had a really close call. She too wanted to look out the window as her siblings did but wasn't quite balanced enough. One day, as my father entered our bedroom, he saw my sister in the process of tipping over out the window. He ran and grabbed her ankles and pulled her in and just sat there on the floor holding her while trying to regain his composure. I came in and saw him sitting there holding my sister and asked him about it. He explained with gasping breath what had almost happened.

Muehldorf holds many special memories for us children. It was there where I entered second grade and was taught by nuns. There was no choice; the nuns were the only game in town. We realized quickly that these nuns were even meaner than the teachers who had taught us before. Besides using the same kind of whip, worse yet, they pinched your arm really hard!

I quickly became aware that I could not read and was generally way behind second-grade level because of the lack of education I had received up until then. Our normal class was held in the mornings, so I decided to attend the afternoon session of the other second-grade class on my own. I didn't even tell my mother; I just did it.

I recall that the afternoon class had a new girl from Helgoland, a small island in the North Sea, who did not speak a word of German and really had to struggle. I was drawn to her in particular, as she and I were in a similar predicament of needing to catch up. Remembering her, I still feel ashamed for the entire class as everyone always snickered when she could not pronounce *sechsundsechzig* (sixty-six). In fact, most of my classmates looked forward to the moment when the teacher would ask her to do so and waited for the struggling result. Children can be so cruel, but in all honesty, the teacher should not have engaged in this game of humiliation.

I did catch up eventually, and one of the nuns actually praised me to my mother, saying that she had never come across such a conscientious child before. From that time on, things were better between the nuns and me. Mutti was equally impressed and oh so proud of me. She would bring this up in conversation many years later and even then would slowly shake her head in admiring amazement. My friend from Helgoland finally succeeded with immense pride in speaking German and was actually able to pronounce *sechsundsechzig* correctly. The class then cheered when it finally happened.

Tante Lis, my father's sister, came to visit us as often as she could. You see, she lived in Communist East Germany. Older people were allowed to cross the border and spend, I believe, up to four weeks a year in West Germany. I know Tante Lis would have loved to stay with us permanently. She was like the grandmother we never knew, but there was at least one major hitch to that plan of her staying with us. Tante Lis had to take care of her ailing sister, Tante Gert, and needed to return to the East for that reason. The government in the DDR (German Democratic Republic) would not have minded too much if she, an older person, had not returned. Older people were not productive and could not contribute to the State and for that reason were of no use to them. If they went to the West, it meant one less person to take care of.

During our early stay in Muehldorf, I recall the daily delivery of hot food by the American military to our school yard. We came with our own cups, containers, and utensils and just lined up to receive whatever hot meal they had for the day. It pretty much was always the same. Most memorable were the green pea soup, thick and laden with ham or bacon (we didn't care which), chicken noodle soup, and oatmeal with raisins or farina. To this day, I can taste this food in my mind and still wouldn't mind having it again.

Once, only once, were we blessed with an honest-to-goodness CARE package from America. My mother proudly placed this treasure chest on the table and opened it slowly. It must have contained products that helped my mother in her effort to feed the family, as she was truly delighted. Too bad I never asked my mother later what exactly was in that package. The most unusual item to us kids was the ice cream powder. We had never tasted ice cream, but the powder mixed with milk tasted awfully good. This was also the time when my sister had her first taste of a chocolate bar. At another time, we were given oranges and bananas, neither of which we had ever seen before. My sister, according to my mother, not knowing what these items were, bit straight into one without first peeling it. The grimace she made was, as you can imagine, comical and priceless.

The times in Muehldorf were better, but we still had to struggle. We were still allotted food stamps until June 20, 1948, when our currency was changed from the Reichsmark to the Deutsche Mark (*Währungsreform,* currency reform).

The Deutsche Mark was introduced by the Western Allies, composed of the U.S.A., the United Kingdom, and France. The intention was to protect West Germany from hyperinflation and to stop the rampant barter and black market trade where, for instance, American cigarettes acted as currency. My parents were perfect examples, as they had fallen victim to the black market quite often to put food on the table and to support their smoking habit. It was a new beginning after years of starvation and having to deal with the corrupt black market in really desperate moments by trading away our valuables for life's necessities.[20] The old Reichsmarks were exchanged for the new currency at a rate of 1 Deutsche Mark to 1 Reichsmark for essentials such as wages, rent payments, etc., and 1 Deutsche Mark to 10 Reichsmarks for the remainder in a private nonbank credit balance. Large amounts (who had it?) were exchanged 10 Reichsmarks to 65 Pfennigs (pennies). In addition, each person received an allowance of 60 Deutsche Marks in two parts: the first being 40 Deutsche Marks and the second being twenty. I remember standing in line with my parents at the town hall, along with the rest of Muehldorf's citizens, to receive our per capita allowance of the new currency. Everyone started off with the preapportioned amount of money and learned to ration their lives dealing with this new currency. It was a new start for everyone, and as history later proved, with perseverance and hard work, Germany became industrious and prosperous again.

When food stamps were still a part of our daily lives before the *Währungsreform*, I remember buying beer at the local brewery in my father's canteen container, which was kidney shaped and was equipped with a handle. The beer was intended for my mother to make her famous creamy beer soup. You may make a face reading this, but I can vouch to you that this sweet soup was most delicious! The same canteen container was also used for purchasing milk. I still feel the pain in my heart when I remember what happened one time.

My mother had given me the very last food stamp for milk and sent me off to the milk store at the other end of town. In one hand, I held the canteen container, and in the other, pressed between my index finger and thumb, was that food stamp. I arrived at the store and had to stand in line for what seemed forever, and then it was my turn. I went on my tippy-toes and handed the woman behind the counter the canteen and requested, "Einen Liter Milch, bitte" (One liter milk, please). Then I lifted the other hand to present the stamp, but it was not there, though my two little fingers were still pressed together. Oh my! They did not give me the milk but sent me on my way.

Slowly I turned back, and my eyes searched the cobblestone street for my lost stamp, but no, there was no stamp to be found. All the way home, I thought of words to explain why the family was not getting milk until the next set of food stamps was issued. I don't recall my mother getting mad; I remember everything else, but no outburst from my mother. Again she showed only compassion for this little girl of hers who was too stressed out as it was. What a woman, my mom!

This does not mean that Mutti didn't paddle us from time to time when, I suppose, we deserved it, like the time in Muehldorf when we lost the only extra key we had while playing on the tree logs piled up at a local sawmill. We just got carried away a bit as we were running along the top logs when Mike slipped and the key around his neck fell between the log spaces. Mike, as you might expect, was mostly on the receiving end of Mutti's discipline. Sometimes it was exacted with the dog leash, but mostly with a wooden spoon—*that* wooden spoon!

The last time I remember having a run-in with that wooden spoon was literally a run-in. We must have done something that aggravated Mutti to no end. We knew what was coming and tried to run away from the punishment. Mutti chased us around the large round dining room table waving that wooden spoon—around and around—until she stopped and broke into laughter. It must have been quite a scene to see herself pursuing her kids around the table wielding a wooden spoon and not making headway. As far as I remember, she did not use that spoon on us again. Many years later when the family emigrated from Germany to the United States, that wooden spoon still existed and was the only utensil that made it across the ocean. I guess it was an heirloom by then, certainly one that we kids will never forget.

After we had moved from Moessling to Muehldorf, we were still invited by the farmer in Moessling, Mr. Niederschreiberer, who was Konrad's father, to pick up food for the family after harvest or slaughter. It was a genuine offer, and Mike and I were again selected to make the journey—on foot, of course. One of those pilgrimages stayed in our minds for many years to come, mainly because our memories were laced with immense guilt. Here is what happened.

We took the long hike to Moessling and were received with friendly hospitality. We were given several food items to take home. Among our treasures was a freshly smoked sausage that had just been taken out of the chimney where the farmer had a special compartment for smoking meat and sausage. As we walked through the tall wheat field, Mike took out his little pocketknife and said, "Just a little sliver off the sausage won't be missed." I was hungry too, so I agreed. It quickly became two slivers and then another and still another. The sausage soon took on a skimpy appearance, too skimpy to bring home to the family. So we finished the whole thing, never telling anyone what we had done. Only years later when we were adults—I believe it was when the family lived in Philadelphia—did we tell the family about it.

It was in Muehldorf when the family began their weekend walks that are such a memorable part of our growing up. Most of the time, we took the ferry across the Inn River and walked through the forest on the other side. My brother Tom has a painting in his home that belonged to my parents, showing tall, strong trees neatly lined up with a path leading straight through them and the sunlight interrupting the uniformity of the trees by angling downward in long, glittering streams. This tranquil, enchanted scene awaited us each time immediately upon getting off the aforementioned ferry as part of our family walks. They are cherished memories indeed.

At other times, we would walk to the end of town, exit through the second city tower gate, cross the bridge, and follow the path along the Inn River in the opposite direction back to the same ferry, which would bring us back home. The ferry, by the way, was operated by an old boatman who stationed himself in a little boathouse on the city side of the river. You had to get his attention to prompt him out of his boathouse to help you across the river. He took his responsibility very seriously and rarely smiled as he handled the long guiding pole, driving it repeatedly into the waters. We kids, of course, snickered behind his back, which at times he noticed and then grumbled something unflattering. We just loved teasing him.

The Inn River, which ran through the town, flooded severely each spring. During flood time, the boat was attached to a cable above so that it would not be carried down the rushing river. One day Mike decided to take that boat— how hard could it be?—and row across, thank God, attached to the cable. The boatman came running out of his house by the river, waving his arms and cursing. I am sure he was also very concerned about Mike, a boy, fighting the rushing waters. Mike made it to one side, where he was greeted by other adults who had been watching this scene unfold. Not only did they prepare a rather damaging report to our parents, but Mike also had to walk all the way downstream until he came to the bridge to return to town center and home. Our parents were waiting for him. Oh, Mike!

Most precious are the memories of our Easter egg walks, also along the riverbanks. The first one was the most exciting, as we had no advance idea of what our parents had planned. Our parents would walk ahead of us, and we followed, usually clowning around or pushing and shoving each other. Then suddenly we would notice colorful Easter eggs or candy on the path. Each time we bent down to collect these treasures, our parents would either drop more or hide others in bushes or on lower tree branches. It was great fun that was repeated each year, and even though we knew what was coming, our parents played the game perfectly.

The scenery for the Easter egg walks was not always the same. Many times the egg hunt took place in our own home because of inclement weather. Just the same, we loved it. We played this family game far into our adulthood and then passed it on to our kids. Many years later when our parents lived in Crestwood Village, New Jersey, their grandchildren were treated to the same surprise Easter egg walk around the nearby Keswick Lake with its seven bridges. Another generation was indoctrinated!

What became of the famous baby carriage that was so indispensable for transporting my sister Sabine and harboring food rations and clothing items when my mother fled Pulsnitz? It was still with us in Muehldorf and had pretty much outlived its usefulness when Mike and Tom (mostly Tom, who had the creative foresight) decided to convert it into a go-cart. They removed the main body from the wheel undercarriage, put a soap box to sit in on top, made some other adjustments and improvements, such as steering and brakes, and off they went to the top of the rather steep hill that rose on one end of the city. A couple of hair-raising trips down the hill with spills and crashes ended that adventure. I wouldn't be surprised if Mike, not listening to Tom's warnings, was behind the demise of this great idea.

Every year on December 5, Germany celebrates Nikolaus Day. On that evening, St. Nikolaus visits children while they sleep and fills their stockings, which are placed in anticipation near their beds, with goodies. The various regions in Germany each have their own traditions.

In Bavaria, it was customary to have a second Nikolaus as a reminder to children with bad behavior: St. Rupprecht. He was there to make sure that the children thought hard about being good. In the late afternoon of December 5, both Nikolauses would stroll down the main marketplace and make a big impression on us kids. In contrast to St. Nikolaus, who was dressed like a bishop with a staff, St. Rupprecht was dressed in burlap rags and swung a chain about him. Oh no, we didn't want to get on the wrong side of him! We chose to quickly retreat to our apartment building into the safety of our home.

After we had returned to our apartment and prepared for bedtime, we heard heavy, firmly placed footsteps coming up the stairs. This was followed by a brief exchange with my parents behind the closed door to our bedroom where we kids hovered, and then the good St. Nikolaus appeared at the doorstep. He was not accompanied by St. Rupprecht—what a relief! We saw a bag slung over his shoulder. After some inquisitorial probing about whether we had been good kids all year—and we nodded eagerly—he took the bag and spilled its contents across the floor. Apples, nectarines, nuts, chocolate, candy—all those things we had been eyeing in the store windows—were now strewn all over our bedroom floor.

Tom, Bine, and I immediately jumped out of our beds to quickly collect whatever we could, but Mike stayed in bed just watching us. My mother asked him later why he hadn't joined us, and he said with wide eyes, "My shirt was too short!" Apparently, he had been wearing the pajama tops while Tom wore the bottoms. Bine and I were luckier; we each wore a long nightgown that my mother had sewn for us. Of course, we shared our loot equally among the four of us.

St. Nikolaus, as we later found out, was the owner of the tobacco store next door, who had suggested this good deed to my parents. Gratefully they had accepted, and it worked like a charm, with all participants feeling very pleased and satisfied. This was just one St. Nikolaus Day in the tradition of many to follow.

We did what German children still do to this day. On the evening of December 5, we placed our empty stockings near the headboards of our beds before going to sleep. In the morning, they were miraculously filled with sweets and nuts and fruits, all of which were very hard to come by. My parents, unbeknown to us, somehow managed to never disappoint us. What an exciting moment it was to wake up the next morning and immediately reach for our stockings and feel the contents that had been placed there overnight—the rustling, the crackling, and the various shapes of mysterious items inside!

Also traditionally, as part of our countdown to Christmas, we each had our own Advent calendar with twenty-four hidden windows to be opened one at a time, starting December 1 and going through December 24, Christmas Eve. Of course, we handed this tradition on to our children and they to our grandchildren. Where it goes from there is hard to tell. The world is changing fast, and what we thought unique, our grandchildren may waste little time even considering. It is up to them to make their own memories—and that's fine too. This account of our history and traditions is simply intended to give a glance into the past and our customs.

9

Life in the Big City

In 1950, we moved to Munich. My father had secured a position with Pan American Airways (PAA), and the big city was to be our new home for the next ten years. On our moving day, with all the scurrying about and excitement, just before we were ready to be on our way, guess who came driving through the city gate with his horse-drawn wagon? Konrad, of all people! He bid us farewell in a very un-Konrad-like manner. This seemingly aloof and cold person, according to our recollection, surprised us with honest upset and sadness when he learned about our intentions. But then he quickly displayed a broad smile and, while hugging each one of us, expressed all good wishes for our future in the big city. Our eyes followed him as he urged his horses to continue his journey through town until he disappeared from view. We had been so wrong about him! We did not know that we would not see him again until forty years later and then another twenty-two years after that.

According to my parents' description, the actual moving trip from Muehldorf to Munich was a hair-raising experience, at least for the adults. We children were actually quite excited about being allowed to sit in the front cabin of one of the two moving trucks together with the driver. What we did not realize was the fact that both drivers were quite intoxicated, even stopping once during the trip at a roadside restaurant/beer garden to top off what was already in excess. They just left us all sitting in the truck and promptly forgot about us. It was very cold and got colder and colder as we waited for their return. After my father went inside to check on them, they reluctantly followed him out, swaying in their every step, and proceeded with the trip, not even offering an apology. My parents, one sitting in each truck, held their breath the entire time, and when the trucks careened down a very long, steep hill (I believe it was the famed Ebersberg hill) without even thinking about braking, they thought the end had come for all of us.

Then came the unloading and delivery of our furniture to the third floor of our new apartment in Munich. Mind you, a floor in Germany is ten feet instead of the American eight. There was no elevator, so they needed to carry every piece up the stairs, around and around. My mother watched as they labored up the stairs, bumping the furniture against either the wall or the banister and, sure enough, breaking almost every glass pane in our credenza and nicking wood surfaces. My parents objected to the treatment of their belongings, but the two drivers got belligerent, and my parents just wanted to get rid of them. In those days, moving trucks were just ordinary trucks, with no padding, no insurance, no liability. You simply paid for the transport, and that was all.

After this ordeal, we began to get accustomed to our new environment in the big city. We kids were registered at school, Flur Schule, and finally got a better and more stable education. Here I again remember one special student who totally impressed me. His last name was Szmuhalek (I am not sure of the spelling), and I don't know from which Slavic country he came; but again, this student did not speak one word of German. He was a quiet, polite student who sat towards the back of the class, near where I was sitting, and once in a while, he would give me a nod of hello or a hint of a smile.

Here is a lesson for all of us: *if you put your mind to it, you can achieve anything.* You see, this student sat in our classroom day after day, listening intently and concentrating on what was being taught up front. Because he had to concentrate so hard, he grasped the curriculum much faster than we did and became the top student in the class. With it, he also became a student who spoke German like the rest of us.

My father became a cargo sales representative for PAA Pan American Airways and needed to be on the road all week long to bring in new accounts or orders for cargo transport on the airline. His accounts primarily dealt with little chicks or agricultural products from Bavaria to be transported to the U.S. For that purpose, he was given a Chevy station wagon with wood-paneled doors advertising the winged emblem of Pan American: PAA.

Surprisingly, one of his assignments had nothing to do with agricultural products but concerned the responsibility to maintain the account of the U.S. Army headquarters at the former POW campsite in Bad Aibling—yes, Bad Aibling. My father's numerous trips on PAA business led him repeatedly to that location. Pan American was the selected airline to transport military personnel and their families, as well as their belongings, to and from the United States. I wonder how he must have felt the first time he returned to the site that some five years earlier had represented the lowest point and such uncertainty in his existence. He never talked about it, although I am sure Mutti and he had their conversations. He merely set out to fulfill the duties of his new job with diligence and perfection. He was liked and respected by all the American military staff, and his success afforded Pan American the resulting business gains.

During the week, the entire family pursued their individual obligations, whether school or work. My mother went back to work to help feed our family of six, but our weekends were spent as a family. Most Saturdays we waited for my father to come home with his pay, which was cash only in those days.

His weekly pay, I believe, was reimbursement for his travel expenses during the week; all regular salaries were paid out on a monthly basis.

My mother had equipped each one of us with a shopping list for a particular store, such as the baker, butcher, fruit and vegetable market, or the grocery store for all the other items. As soon as we had money in hand, off we all went, each in a different direction, to catch the stores open till 2:00 p.m. Sometimes it got a little hairy with little time available. We each had a crocheted shopping net in a different color to carry out this group effort. A shopping net was one of the crafts we girls learned to create in home economics class at school. I made many in my time—just name a color!

We didn't have fancy meals, as meat was either too expensive or scarce. Believe it or not, our favorite meals consisted of spaghetti mixed with ketchup (don't make a face until you have tried it yourself) and rolled up boiled ham, hot rice pudding with cinnamon sugar and browned butter drizzled over it, noodle or potato casseroles, or even simply hot chocolate and buttered rolls or farina with applesauce.

Liver was one of the cheapest cuts of meat. The cheapest yet was cow udder, which we sometimes bought in slices. Mutti would bread and panfry them, and as I remember, it was not bad at all. Sometimes my father would bring home a chicken from his trips through the countryside when he visited the various chicken farms for his business. One roasted chicken divided between six hungry mouths was not much, but we just relished those occasions.

Casseroles were on our menu often, as they easily fed and satisfied our family of six. When we kids came home from school, our favorite snack was a slice of dark bread with butter and sugar—yes, sugar! How scrumptious it was to bite into the slice and hear and feel the crunchy sugar. Later, after my mother went back to work, we would find thermos containers filled with delicious hot food on the kitchen table. She was indeed the ultimate mother hen. Thanks, Mutti. We loved it.

On our birthdays, we were allowed to choose our favorite meal, and it was almost always fried liver with onions, mashed potatoes, and garden (*Rapunzel*) salad. Mutti also baked a cake for the birthday child, and it was always the same: a vanilla Bundt cake with fudge glazing and one layer of marmalade filling inside. This cake and our birthday gift were placed on our night table in the morning before we woke up. In my case, since I was born in April, a pot with hyacinths was added, and its sweet pungent scent was the immediate cause of my waking up.

After my mother went back to work, my parents felt that there should be some domestic help and supervision for us children. Two young ladies (to us, of course, they seemed old) were hired in succession. The first one, Christa, certainly had our affection, while Erna, the second one, definitely rubbed us the wrong way with her brash attitude and disinterested demeanor. She did not last long, and we were on our own again. No problem—we had been raised well and knew how to handle our daily routines.

Our apartment was very basic. We had no refrigerator, only a very small chamber where we could store our perishables, though not for too long during the hot summer. There was also no bathtub. Once a week, my mother would pull in an aluminum tub, place it in the middle of the kitchen, which was the only warm room, and fill it with hot water boiled on the wood-burning stove in the kitchen and topped with cold water to equalize the temperature. One after the other, we children took our baths and thought it was wonderful. Later, as we got older, we went to the nearby public *Brausebad* (shower bathhouse). For a minimal fee, you could get your own shower stall and really clean up in privacy and to your liking.

The famous trunk stood in the entry hallway. Besides still serving as a storage place, it was also my father's resting spot after he struggled up the three flights of stairs when returning from work in the city or from one of his out-of-town trips. His asthma was now clearly a health factor. We all knew not to rush to greet him but waited until he was finished getting his breath back by literally hanging over the top of the trunk for several long minutes. How sad—remember the desperate tobacco-growing episode in Muehldorf?

We lived directly behind the Catholic cathedral Johanniskirche and quickly were 'christened' to listen to and actually enjoy the church bells that rang every evening and especially on Sundays and holidays. There is nothing like the sound of those European church bells, especially in Bavaria, whether in the city or in some mountain village. On special holidays, such as Corpus Christi or Palm Sunday, we watched the church processions pass right below our window. We found them most interesting because they were so different from anything we did in our church, Lutheran Evangelical, my father's faith.

We all had many friends from school in our immediate neighborhood. We spent our free time playing ball against the wall of the windowless side of the apartment building on the next street, marbles, hopscotch, or hide-and-seek in the many niches of Johanniskirche or the park on both sides of the church. On many occasions, we walked along the Isar River, which fascinated us immensely, especially during flood season when the snow and ice had melted in the mountains and the swelling waters came rushing through our town. Once my brother Mike persuaded us siblings to walk out on the breaker wall that was strategically constructed diagonally into the river to slow down the wild waters as they came rushing through town. Needless to say, we never told our parents about it, once again, until later when we were adults.

We also belonged to a youth group called the GYO, German Youth Organization, which had been founded by the Americans for us German youngsters. Our original meetings took place in the building of what is now the Hofbräukeller in Munich-Haidhausen. Later we utilized the building and grounds of what ultimately became the Reitschule in Schwabing. It was a great time of socializing and playing games with youngsters of our own age under the guidance of the Americans or their German-speaking counterparts. We put on shows and musicals and visited the Amerika Haus in Munich, which displayed and represented life in the U.S.A.

In summer, we went to the local swimming pool or went roller skating along our sidewalks; and in winter, we went sleigh riding down a steep hill near the Maximilianaeum, the parliament building nearby. We were never bored, though we had no television or computers, and electronic gadgets had not yet been invented. On cold winter evenings, we would sit around the coal/wood-burning stove in our living room and read, do needlework, or chat. On Sunday afternoons, the family would play card games, mostly rummy, and listen to radio programs, such as *Mystery Theater*, in German. One memorable show was *Patricia and the Jewels*, for which we gathered around the radio in impatient anticipation once a week. The suspense which lingered throughout the following week till the next episode seemed unbearable. Sometimes we listened to AFN, the Armed Forces Network.

The coals for our stove needed to be hand-carried up the three flights (actually four in total) from the basement, where each tenant had a space for storage. The coals were delivered by truck and dropped through a window shoot to the basement and then split up between the tenants. Thinking of these basements gives me a very chilling feeling as I remember how a school friend of mine, Sigrun Kastl, was brutally murdered as she went to fetch coal so she and her father would be warm.

Sigrun's mother had died years earlier, and she lived on the third floor of the apartment building with her father, who on that day was still at work. Sigrun merely wanted to surprise her father by taking over this chore so he would not have to upon returning from work. A tenant who lived on the bottom floor followed her into the basement after she passed his door, with the intent to rape her. She fought so fiercely that he resorted to grabbing a nearby axe and killing her. She was only sixteen years old.

Sigrun and I had walked home from school that day, done homework together in the afternoon, and planned to meet the next morning to again walk to school. When I showed up at her apartment door the following morning to pick her up, I was told by a sobbing relative that she was dead. That shocking and sad incident will never leave my mind. Sigrun was a cheerful and full of life 16-year old who was liked and loved by so many. She never had a chance in life, how sad. Rest in peace, Sigrun.

Sigrun and I attended Riemerschmid Handelsschule, the only higher education school solely sponsored and funded by the city of Munich. It was an all-girls school that prepared us for various professions in commerce and was renowned throughout Munich's corporate world. This was my only chance for higher education as my parents could not afford to send me to any tuition-based school. The pressure was almost overwhelming when I headed to the entrance examination. It was extraordinarily difficult, and prospective students were filtered through with tight scrutiny. Because the school was free, my particular entrance exam attracted nine hundred hopefuls.

After the exam, my father accompanied me back to the location where we had taken our test to learn whether or not I had passed. He was sitting next to me, squeezed sideways onto the small school bench with his knees sticking out into the aisle—my father, this tall, handsome, and dignified man! Since my name always appeared close to the beginning of the alphabet, we found out very quickly, and after we heard the good news, my father reached over and squeezed my hand hard. Leaving the classroom, he proudly wrapped one arm around my shoulders. How proud was he! Quite honestly, so was I and I seemed to float in my step on the way home.

Approximately 400 of the 900 applicants were accepted into the school, and after a three-month probationary period, perhaps only half of us remained to complete the three-year program with a diploma. By Christmas of the first school year, our class consisted of 44 students, 17 of which were questionable to continue. By graduation three years later, our class had dwindled to 28 students. Without exception, each of the graduates held a job offer in her hands before leaving the school to enter the business world. You see, corporations approached the school to pick their new employees from the graduating classes before the end of each school year—not the other way around. Attending the fiftieth anniversary reunion of our class in 2006, I learned that while the school now operates under an updated, modern curriculum, it still maintains the same reputation. That's very satisfying to know.

Christmastime was always special. My parents upheld the custom of hanging an Advent wreath from our lamp over the dining room table. My father wove broad red ribbons around the wreath and placed onto it four red candles that were then lighted on each of the Advent Sundays preceding Christmas. The lighting was done ceremoniously by my father after dinner. As we watched the candles burn, we reflected on this special holiday and enjoyed cookies and slices of the traditional Christmas *Stollen* (the recipe is a Dresden original) my mother had baked. It was always very festive.

Then came Christmas itself. Oh, the wish lists, the secrets, the anticipation, my parents' whispering in English behind our backs because they knew we could not understand what they were saying! In those days, we handcrafted gifts for each other, which really meant a lot to the recipient. I still have a Christmas tablecloth that I embroidered for my parents, all the while trying not to be seen in the process of completing it. After my mother passed away, I took the tablecloth back, and with sweet memories, I now place it on our own coffee table each year. I recall that on the night before that particular Christmas, December 24, I waited for my parents to go to sleep so I could finish the lace edging and then wash and dry the tablecloth by hand. I placed the tablecloth near the potbellied stove in the living room and held my breath that neither of my parents would wander in the next morning before I could hide it again. The surprise worked the way I had hoped, although I thought the cloth still felt a bit damp after my parents unwrapped it.

Christmas Eve went as follows: We children went to the Lutheran church while my parents stayed home to prepare. One beautiful memory that will always be with us is the time it snowed while we were in church. We stepped out of the church into a white winter wonderland. The world around us was so breathtakingly still, and our shoes made a crunching sound in the freshly fallen snow.

Upon our arrival home, we found our parents still behind the locked living room door. We heard shoving, crackling, and rustling coming from the other side, and we were bursting with anxiety. After a while, which was far too long for us, we were allowed inside. There we saw for the first time our Christmas tree, fully decorated and illuminated with real candles. The candles were clamped to the branches of the tree, making sure that the branch above was far enough away not to catch on fire. For that reason, the trees in those days looked a bit skimpier than the ones we know now, since more open space around the lit candles was required. This practice of real candles on Christmas trees is still upheld and so far has not been outlawed in Germany.

The sight of the lighted Christmas tree put us immediately into a festive mood, and then we spotted the gifts underneath it! We immediately noticed the *one* gift we had been hoping for and wanted to run right to it to hold it, but no, we were first required to stand in front of the tree and sing at least one Christmas song together. I believe we chose "Ihr Kinderlein Kommet," or "Stille Nacht, Heilige Nacht." Whichever one we chose, it was the longest song *ever*. We then rushed to our specific gift, and we were in heaven. A sled, a pair of ice skates, a doll or dollhouse, an Erector set, or a pair of boots—there was *one* gift per person, and we were happy.

Besides the one gift for each member of the family, our parents always prepared for each child a separate platter that held an apple, mandarins, nuts, a banana, *Pfeffernuesse* and *Lebkuchen* cookies, chocolate, and hard candy. After the exchange of gifts, we sat down for dinner, which was very simple yet special to us. We enjoyed Mutti's famous herring salad, a family recipe, and rolled up boiled ham slices, followed by hot chocolate and *Stollen* and *Spekulatius* cookies. When the evening was over, my parents carefully smothered the candles on our tree. The scent from the smoldering wicks was heavenly and was and always will be a part of the Christmases we knew and loved. We children went to bed with our gifts under our arms, as well as the personal plates with goodies prepared by our parents, and placed them next to our beds where we could find these treasures immediately upon waking the next morning.

On Christmas Day, our festive meal consisted of the traditional Christmas goose with red cabbage and dumplings. I close my eyes and remember the aroma that drifted through our apartment as this meal was prepared and the scrumptious, flavorful meal that followed. A goose is very fatty, and the drippings were collected during the roasting process. The rendered and hardened form was later spread on dark bread with a sprinkle of salt. Oh, to die for!

I believe it was our first Christmas in Munich in 1950 when my father was extended an invitation by the American military to bring his wife and children to a Christmas party at the officer's home near one of Munich's U.S. military barracks. I suspect that my father's affiliation with Pan American was the association to this invitation. Excitedly we went, and I can only describe our (the children's) impression of this event.

We entered a large room and saw a Christmas tree from floor to ceiling ablaze with what seemed like hundreds of colorful lights. The floor beneath it displayed an abundance of gifts, and we were very intrigued. The adults were all dressed very festively and gathered in an adjoining room while we kids lingered around the tree eyeing the presents. Then came the *Bescherung*, handing out of the gifts. I never forgot my present, a glass sewing machine filled with tiny colorful sprinkle candies. I believe my sister's was a glass bell, and my brothers got glass motorcycles or trucks, all filled with the same candy delight. We also received a holiday bag packed with delightful sweets. The most thrilling items were the rolls of Lifesavers in multiple colors, which we had never seen before. We were thrilled and clutched our possessions even during the dinner that followed.

We children were placed in a separate room, and throughout dinner we noticed a bowl in the center of the table with large white balls. We thought they were decorations and would not have dreamt of touching them. Had we known that they were marshmallows to be placed into our hot chocolate, this would have been another highlight of the evening. Now, as an adult in the U.S., every time I see these "white balls" in the super-market, I remember and smile.

Though we were somewhat confined in the winter, the summer months made up for it. As mentioned earlier, Pan American had assigned a station wagon to my father, and although my father was driving all week long, he never tired of taking the family to the mountains, the Alps, every Sunday. We were the only family in our neighborhood that had a car, and we were watched with envious eyes every time we set out on one of our many trips into the countryside. A one or two hour drive would bring us to the foot of a specific mountain, where we would park the car and set out to hike upwards over flowering meadows to a rustic lodge, or *Alm*. Here we would stop and take in refreshments in the form of milk, cheese, and bread, and for my parents, perhaps a small beer. On especially hot days, we dipped our forearms into the ice cold water of a hollowed tree trunk outside a lodge through which cold mountain water flowed.

Many weekends we chose to walk in the forests outside of Munich, such as Grünwald. We had a miniature dachshund then; her name was Trixie. She came along on all our walks, which is really remarkable considering her short legs and the many steps she had to take to match ours.

Walks in Grünwald with Trixie

Trixie was a true family dog and enjoyed going places with us. She was a character, though. More than a few times, she gave us some moments to remember. Once, during one of our mountain hikes, she took off and disappeared into a henhouse at a nearby mountain farm. We sent Mike to get her. He went, but all he could report was, "I can't. She is eating the chickens!" At that we all fled in different directions to avoid the farmer's wrath, and out came Trixie with a mouthful of chicken feathers. At the sight of that, we all retreated even faster, followed by Trixie still decorated with those feathers.

At other times, we watched with disgust and repulsion as Trixie would first spot a cow pie ahead, then start running towards it and just before reaching it flip over on her back and slide through it. Each time we knew what was coming, but calling out to her simply had no effect. She was on a mission. And when it was all over, we swore we could see a smile on her face as she had completed this task. The ride home in the car was anything but pleasant, to say the least—six humans and a smelly little dog!

We all hold such long-lasting memories of those mountain hikes, each location having a story to tell. Our joyful strolls took us over sloping mountain meadows laden with a colorful array of wild flowers. On rare occasions, we were able to see two types of alpine flowers growing openly: the dark blue, almost purplish, *Enzian* (gentian) and pink *Almrausch* (alpine glow); however we found no *Edelweiss*. These velvety white rosettes are generally found in altitudes from 1,700 to 2,700 meters in calcareous soil tucked into cracks of steep mountain rock.

Edelweiss was long valued as the ultimate love charm of the mountains. Love-struck young men tried to endear themselves by collecting *Edelweiss* from those hard-to-access crags and ledges in the High Alps. During these quests, many died from falls or succumbed to exposure, being insufficiently prepared for sudden weather changes. The danger-wrought exercise of collecting such a bouquet proved in those days that the suitor was brave, able-bodied, and serious in his intentions. In conjunction with the governments of Austria, Switzerland, Germany, and Italy, the *Edelweiss* was declared protected in a large part of the European Alps in 1878. By that time, it had already disappeared along the more popular hiking and climbing routes. The *Enzian* and *Almrausch* were placed under protection as well. We never picked these alpine flowers as we had been told that they were protected and we dutifully adhered to these instructions. However, we picked colorful bouquets of the other wild flowers gathered in the sloping mountain meadows. They ultimately made their way home with us, the stems carefully wrapped in one of my father's handkerchiefs, wetted down in a mountain brook or the hollowed out tree trunk near a lodge.

While most of our excursions into the mountains were cheerful and pleasant experiences, there was one occasion that still causes us to shudder just remembering it. On that particular Sunday, our chosen location was the quaint village of Reit-im-Winkel and the many hiking trails that originated from there. We set out with glee upward over meadows with the plan to return via a path that drew a circle back to the village. Fairly high up this path, we were unexpectedly brought to a cliff, and we had to make a choice: turn around or continue by traversing over a narrow ledge by holding on to a cable and sidestepping across. It was certainly the shortest way home, and the day was already growing short. So the entire family stepped out onto the ledge and inched their way across, facing the rock wall while grasping the cable for dear life. And all along, our miniature dachshund, Trixie, excitedly ran back and forth at the cliff's edge; in her mind she was herding our family. No-one spoke as we all had to deal with our own concentrated effort to make it across alive. The only sound which could be heard were the short exhausted puffs of breath of our little dog and her tiny paws scraping along the edge – back and forth.

Later we learned that several members of our family had a really tough time during this ordeal. My father could not handle heights because of the eardrum injury he had received during the war. My mother realizing my father's distress, tried to help him across while clutching the cable and at the same time keeping an eye on her children. My brother Mike had a similar problem of defective equilibrium caused by childhood middle ear infections and had to grit his teeth in desperation. In retrospect, we all had a guardian angel, there is no doubt.

During our mountain hikes, there were moments when we simply held our breath in astonishment when confronted with the incredible beauty of our surroundings, the Bavarian Alps. Standing on top of a mountain, whether it is achieved by climbing, hiking, or by cable car, is always without fail an inspiring moment, no matter how many times you experience it. It was always awe-inspiring to see the mountain chain stretched before our eyes in massive gray topped with intermittent snow, even in the summer. Green meadows and forests spread across the terrain below the gray rock walls like raggedy carpets strewn about, and tiny-looking villages nestled safely in the valley, their individual houses surrounding the village church with its pointed steeple. Sometimes the sound of church bells would drift upward to fill the air to complete the serene atmosphere. At such moments, you realize the greatness and majesty of God's creation. You have the sensation of being close to heaven and are convinced that if you prayed, God would answer you directly right then and there. My parents certainly felt it. We children did not quite understand it but instinctively yielded to this phenomenon and stood in awe each time.

At other times, we children had a hard time being quiet participants. We laughed and joked and clowned around, Mike being the instigator most times, but never so loudly as to miss the constant reassuring clanging of the cowbells reaching our ears in the background from various mountain meadows around us. What a beautiful, peaceful sound! Once in a while, you could even hear honest-to-goodness yodeling by a local who just felt like expressing his or her joy this way. Yes, this really does happen, not just in the movies. It is that moment of serenity that beckoned my parents and later us children as adults back to that region over and over again.

It is astonishing to realize that our father endured all those mountain hikes even though his labored breathing was a constant issue. He did it for the love of his family. Thank you, Vati. You gave us an irreplaceable gift to take into our future.

My father at Eckbauer, Garmisch

My parents also took daily walks after dinner through the English Garden in Munich, usually to the *Friedensengel* (Angel of Peace) statue overlooking Prinzregenten Strasse, and back. When we were smaller, we accompanied them, but later as we got older, we spent those short early evening hours with our friends before it was time to meet the curfew set by our parents, which we dutifully observed. Only once in a while would we go with them, and when we did, we were always treated to Italian ice from the *Eisdiele* (ice cream parlor) on the way home, or we stopped at the Hofbraeukeller, one of the most authentic beer gardens in Munich besides the Hofbraeuhaus. My parents enjoyed their beer and white radish, and we were treated to *Wienerwurst* or Munich *Weisswurst*.

10

East Germany
(DDR: German Democratic Republic)

After we moved to Munich in 1950, my father was promoted to the position of cargo manager for Pan American World Airways. PAA was one of the three airlines that were allowed to fly to Berlin in the designated air corridor over East German territory. The other two were British Air and Air France. We children often had the privilege of flying to Berlin during our summer vacation. Our Tante Ali, my mother's sister, who had survived the bombardments and difficult times in Berlin, still lived there, and we loved to visit with her.

Landing in Berlin was wonderfully exciting to us kids as the plane needed to fly low over the roof tops of the city in order to quickly set down at the airport located smack in mid-city. Many pilots had expressed to my father how they felt about landing in Berlin as one of the more difficult to approach of all the airports worldwide, Hong Kong being one other. We children, of course, enjoyed the spectacle of seeing people walking in the streets as we flew over.

After the end of World War II in Europe, what remained of Germany west of the Oder-Neisse line was divided into four occupation zones in accordance with the Potsdam

Agreement. Each territory was controlled by one of the four occupying Allied powers: the Americans, British, and French in the west, and the Soviet Union in the east.

Berlin was similarly subdivided into four sectors, despite the city lying deep inside the Soviet zone. The city was an island surrounded entirely by the Soviet Union. Berlin remained this Western island for forty-five years until the unification of the two Germanys on October 3, 1990. It withstood immense difficulties and pressures in the early years following the war; in particular, a land-and-water blockade of the city instituted by the Soviet Union in the hope that the Allies would be forced to abandon West Berlin. On the contrary, in June 1948, primarily under U.S. auspices, the Berlin Airlift began to supply vital necessities to West Berlin by air transport. This massive effort to supply two million West Berliners with food and coal for heating was accomplished with an around-the-clock airlift that lasted until September 1949. It included 277,000 flights, many in three-minute intervals, transporting an average of eight thousand tons daily.

One year after the famous Berlin Airlift which saved the population of the western part of the former German capital from starvation, America presented a special gift to the people of Berlin in form of the Freedom Bell. This ten-ton bell was designed after the Liberty Bell in Philadelphia as a symbol of the common fight for freedom and against the threat of Communism. Some seventeen million Americans had donated the funds for this special gift. It rang for the first time on October 24, 1950 from the clock tower of City Hall in Schöneberg, West Berlin and subsequently on special occasions, such as the revolt of the workers in East Germany (June 17, 1953), during the Hungarian Revolution (1956), during the construction of the infamous Berlin Wall (1961), and of course in celebration of the reunification of Germany (1990). This bell is still in use today and reached the ears and hearts of the population following the terror attacks on the World Trade Center on September 11, 2001.[21]

Visiting the divided Berlin in the fifties was an experience that left us kids with some troubling memories. Whenever we walked anywhere, we came upon barricades and warning signs indicating that beyond a certain point, we would be leaving either the American or British sector and would be entering the eastern, or Russian, zone. We were too afraid to take a bus or underground and instead walked everywhere just to avoid inadvertently winding up in the Russian zone.

A visit to Wannsee, a famous lake recreation spot in Berlin that is visited by families as a getaway for relaxation and water sports, presented the senselessness of the division in clear view. We were told to look across the water and we would see the east zone (*Ostzone*) and that the swimmers and boats on the other side were all in the east zone. Leave it to children to wonder where they drew the line in the water!

A sad testimony of the Communists' interference with the human desire to live in freedom or at least to communicate with family members on the other side (East and West) was demonstrated in 1961. It had become apparent that people trapped in East Germany were fleeing to the West in droves. To stop this flow of defections and to prevent East Berliners from commuting to the West, a border was erected. At first constructed of barbed wire along the border between East and West Berlin, the barrier was eventually replaced by a concrete structure—the Berlin Wall—that was topped with barbed wire and studded with watchtowers manned by East German guards.

It was then observed by the East German guards that families and friends would wave to each other across the wall at certain times, mostly on Sundays. To accomplish this, they strategically selected various elevated locations to actually see their counterparts on the other side. As a result, a second wall was erected, which was even higher, and a minefield and barbed wire were laid between the two walls. A deep trench was dug in front of the wall on the East side in an effort to prevent any attempt to flee by car. The apartment buildings that were located along the wall continued to serve as escape places where desperate defectors jumped out of windows onto sidewalks to gain freedom. Those buildings were subsequently bricked up to permanently close off East Berlin.

The most heartbreaking escape witnessed by the world was the attempt of a teenager to flee to the West, only to be shot by the East German border guards and left lying on a ledge ironically called the "death strip." Eighteen-year-old Peter Fechter bled to death on August 17, 1962, in full view of the Western media, and no one had the guts to intervene. I too watched it on the news in New York and felt total disbelief and disgust. Fechter's death created negative publicity worldwide that led the leaders of East Berlin to place more restrictions on shooting in public places and to provide medical care for would-be escapees, but it was too late for Peter.

In 1964, my husband and I traveled to Berlin by air to visit with Tante Ali. During our stay, we took a bus tour through West Berlin, along the wall, and then to East Berlin by way of Checkpoint Charlie. We saw with breaking hearts the infamous wall and the bricked-up buildings where flower bouquets and other memorials had been placed on the sidewalk to remember those individuals who had not survived their attempts to flee to freedom.

If we had been depressed by seeing the wall, Checkpoint Charlie was yet another unsettling moment. The bus was halted, and our Western tour guide had to leave and was replaced with an East German guide. Our passports had to be surrendered, something you never, ever want to do when you are on foreign soil, even today. Your passport is your only hope to reconnect with your homeland, should something go awry. Luckily, I did not have my own passport but was included on my husband's U.S. passport. This way no one knew that I had been born in East German territory.

The bus was searched with Geiger counters all around and underneath, and throughout all this antagonistic theater, we were being observed with field binoculars from the tall buildings nearby. I have one of those authentic binoculars used at the Berlin Wall in my possession, a 7 x 40 power with night vision. After a deliberately long wait, the bus left, now with our new guide, and we were taken along Stalin Allee. Here the intent was to show off the Communist architecture of boxy concrete buildings, which were not very impressive, and the many storefronts that displayed items the ordinary citizen could not dream of purchasing.

I have always been a people watcher, and on that excursion in particular, I observed the people walking about. Most of them were poorly dressed, slumped over, with blank, hopeless expressions on their faces. I felt so guilty for my cushy life in the United States.

Our bus continued to the Stalin Memorial. At that location, we were actually allowed to disembark the bus and walk around the monument. All around us were East German guards with German shepherds or vicious-looking Dobermans on a tight leash, and they followed every step we took. Needless to say, we were glad to get back on the bus and head back to the West, hoping all along that we would get our passports back. We did—what a relief! The tour guides were exchanged once more, and the bus returned to the depot from which the tour had originated. My husband and I were so depressed coming away from this experience that we could not talk for hours, each of us wrapped up in our own emotions.

Throughout the years following the end of World War II, East Germany remained untouched, in somber, gray display of the defeat suffered in 1945 and subsequent take-over by the Soviet Union, while West Germany underwent extensive reconstruction. And then it happened. In 1989, a massive exodus of East German families was initiated after the Hungarian government removed the border restrictions between Hungary and Austria. This was the first piece of the Iron Curtain, so named by Winston Churchill in the late forties, to come tumbling down. Thousands of East Germans started to flee westward via Hungary and on through Austria. It started when family after family had the well thought-out plan to travel south to these countries during school vacation and then, instead of returning home, defect from there to the West. Hungary and Austria suddenly had their hands full but handled this humanitarian effort with diligence and compassion.

The growing flow of refugees could not be ignored by the powers up north. As a result, the beleaguered East German regime lifted travel restrictions in early November of 1989, and days later, with East German guards looking on helplessly, the wall was dismantled. The tumbling of the Berlin Wall on November 9, 1989, and the reunification of the two Germanys on October 3, 1990, brought about the long overdue freedom to the citizens of former East Germany who had lived under the Soviet yoke for forty-five years.

While citizens in West Germany had the freedom to strive and achieve and rebuild, East Germans were trapped and swallowed up by the oppressive Soviet-East German regime and were kept under strict control and supervision. Productivity of any East German worker was a group effort rather than an individual endeavor. All productivity was solely for the good of the State, which owned you, body and soul.

The East German government purposefully created a so-called bible that formulated guidelines under socialism for the East German worker. It was called *Die Politische Oekonomie des Sozialismus und ihre Anwendung in der DDR (The Political Economy of Socialism and Its Application in the*

DDR (Deutsche Demokratische Republik). The old people in the DDR who were no longer productive were dispensable and could leave the State, if they so chose. Remember the case for my two aunts, Tante Lis and Tante Gert.

By the time East and West Germany were reunited, the people of East Germany consisted of those who still remembered life before the Soviet takeover and who subsequently had to conform and submit to their new authority, and the younger East Germans who had grown up under the Communist regime and knew no other life. Some of the younger generation, though, within time had become aware that there was a better way, as they heard stories and news reports trickling in from the outside (the West) as well as listening to the remembrances of their elders. They began to question their existence under Soviet law, and a simmering underground revolt was eventually in the making.

It is also understandable that a certain degree of resentment or underlying sense of abandonment immerged on the side of many East Germans towards their capitalist brothers and sisters in West Germany while they remained captive and trapped under Communist oppression. During those long years since the Communist takeover and continuing through the Cold War, nothing much happened on the international political stage to bring about change to this situation. But then President Kennedy visited Berlin and made his famous "Ich bin ein Berliner" speech on June 26, 1963; and twenty-four years later, on June 12, 1987, President Reagan made his even more famous request to the Russians: "Mr. Gorbachev, tear down this wall!" This finally had the necessary impact to get things moving. The outcome is now history.

As much as the majority of East Germans had dreamt of freedom from oppression, the ultimate changeover to life in a Western capitalist civilization was in the beginning quite difficult. Old and young alike suddenly had to learn a new way of life. No one wanted to go back to the days of dictatorship, but at the same time, they were not happy with the new system. It was full of challenges for which they were totally unprepared. Many wished they had not been forced to give up job security, blanket social guarantees, and other state-sponsored aspects of the lives they had lived before 1989. That's what socialism does: it robs you of your own initiative and stifles creativity, individualism, and promotion of self. There is no self—only the State.

Many years have passed since then, and the two Germanys have blended well and are now experiencing life, good or bad, as one nation. They have found their self and are now striving forward along with their brothers and sisters of long ago.

11

Big Decisions

Munich 1950–1958
We were a very close-knit family and lived our lives in the comfort of a warm and secure unity of love and contentment, even during meager and rough times. We loved doing things together, and we were not only admired but also secretly envied by our friends and neighbors.

The Bierling family in Munich—1954
(Note cigarette in my mother's hand.)

Then, in late 1957, my parents became interested in the possibility of living in America. This awakening interest in the U.S.A. was actually fostered by my father's boss, who was being transferred back to the States and who had suggested that my father and his family should think about doing the same. My father investigated Hialeah, Florida, as Pan American had their hub there, and he was told that there could be a job for him. We set into motion the emigration process through the American consulate.

It took one long year of going through rigorous and thorough personal, political, and medical checkups and investigation. It was very nerve-racking for my parents because the scrutiny was intense. My mother had worked for a charitable emigration organization with a quota system years earlier, and she had seen much heartbreak and disappointment because of some minor infraction of one or another family member's part disqualifing that individual from entry into the United States. With the rejection of that one member, the rest of the family decided in the end not to go. Many never made it through the medical examination. In our case, towards the end of our investigation and after clearing everything else, it was discovered that my father's chest x-rays showed spots on his lungs. Our hopes sank! He was required to undergo further detailed scanning to search deeper for clarification. We too had our suspicions. You see, my father had been diagnosed with asthma three years earlier. He had suffered from shortness of breath for a long time.

When I was sixteen, my father had been sent to Bad Reichenhall for a saline cure, and he was told that if he did not quit smoking, he had perhaps a year to live. He gave up this habit immediately, but his breathing did not improve, and now the American authorities had discovered something wrong with his lungs. As it turned out, the spots were merely inactive lung chambers that were filled with dead air. Finally, he too got his clearance after all. We were proudly issued our six visas, and everyone was very excited and dreamed in his or her own way about the new life we would have in America.

In Berlin, my mother's sister, Tante Ali, decided to come with us and put in her application for emigration from Germany to the U.S. Here I need to mention that anyone wishing to emigrate had to observe the appropriate quotas for the respective country of birth. Now this became interesting, since my mother had been born in China and Tante Ali in Kobe, Japan. Therefore, we were placed in three different quota systems: my father and we children were carried under Germany/white; my mother, under China/white; and my aunt, under Japan/white. Besides worrying about my father's medical approval, we were very nervous about how my mother's application was coming along. Finally, we were very relieved when she, along with the rest of our family, was approved.

It so happened that the Japanese quota was exhausted, and my aunt had to stay back. How disappointing that was. She continued to live in Berlin with her only family members thousands of miles away.

Tante Ali's full name was Alice Decarli. Did you notice the link to the Decarli stage name? She was an actress on the theatre stage as well as film and later made immeasurable contributions to radio broadcasting at Radio RIAS Berlin. She had an incredible speaking voice that clearly stood out and caused you, the listener, to wish she would just go on and never stop.

We always loved listening to her reading stories, as she presented them with such animation, mimicking each character to perfection; it was almost a play in itself. Often during our visits in Berlin, we loved to listen to her rehearsing her script prior to her appearances on Radio RIAS and then remained in her apartment after she left for work at the radio station and listened to her live programs with the same fascination. The summers we spent with her are precious memories filled with so many special moments of learning and laughter.

Mutti and I loved to go to the movies and watch all those American flicks that were dubbed in German. They usually played late at night—11:00 p.m.—at one particular theater near our home, and it was always great fun to sneak out and walk through echoing, empty streets to go to the movie theater. On one of those occasions, we were listening quite intently to one particular dubbed voice; it seemed so familiar. At the end, we got our answer as we read the credits and saw my aunt's name, Alice Decarli, scrolling by. Her life achievements can be found on wikipedia – Alice_Decarli. She is another family member we can be so proud of. [22]

Although Alice was surrounded by a large circle of friends and colleagues who respected and admired her, they were no substitute for family. Some years later, Alice became very ill with cancer. After an excruciatingly long fight trying to conquer this disease, she passed away in 1964 with her sister, my mother, by her side. She was a very special person and we still miss her.

I would like to add that after our approval, each member of our family required two U.S. sponsors who would vouch for our good character and take responsibility for us once we arrived in the United States. This one-year sponsorship was required by U.S. immigration law. There were two gentlemen from Pan American who stepped forward on our behalf: Mr. Ernest Wood and Mr. Anthony Bernaccia, both of Long Island. What has happened to those immigration laws over the years since then? I will address this phenomenon later.

As mentioned earlier, our original plan was to make our home and my father's professional seat in Miami/Hialeah, a Pan American hub. This location in warmer climate was so promising to my father and his health condition. Everything was set, and we were ready to go. We were all very excited and started to make plans for a new beginning in that mysterious new land called the United States of America. However, a short time later, upsetting news came from our Pan American contacts about reorganization within PanAm and the reassignments and layoff of many of their workers, as well as the possibility of a lengthy strike. It was therefore strongly suggested that my father not come to the States under these tenuous circumstances. My father was told: "We cannot justify bringing you over here from another country while this is going on." There was no time frame given nor a hopeful "try again a little later" encouragement. Therefore, the decision was made to abort our emigration. Oh my— such disappointment and tears!

We told the American consul that we would not make use of our visas and would stay in Munich. The consul was surprised and puzzled as well, as he knew of the slim chances of six members of one family making it through the ultimate test of the immigration process. He told my parents the following: "This is highly unusual and off the record. I will keep your six visas in your file for one year. If you decide within that time to go after all, just come to my office and pick them up. Good luck!"

It so happened that a former colleague of my father, Rolf L., who had moved to New York a number of years prior, heard about our situation. He worked for the German-American Tourist Information Office on Fifth Avenue in New York. His office was looking for a bilingual secretary-assistant, and he telegraphed my father to ask whether I would be interested, since I had all the qualifications. He also knew that I had my visa ready; I just needed to hop on a plane and come over. My father read the telegram to me over the phone while I was at work. My answer was quick and simple: "Yes, I'll do it." And so, at age nineteen, I was the first one of our family to figuratively fly the coop.

The letter on file to the U.S. consulate general in Munich, written by Ernest Wood, our sponsor, reads as follows:

Dear Sirs,
In connection with sponsoring Mr. Alfred Bierling and his entire family for emigration, I am now advised that Mr. Bierling's daughter Gisela, aged 19, plans to emigrate by herself in order to take up employment at the German Tourist Office here in New York on or about January 5, 1959.

This is to confirm that I am prepared to sponsor Miss Bierling on an individual basis.
Needless to say, I would be indebted to you for expeditious handling of the visa issuance, which will allow Miss Bierling to start her new job on the appointed date.

Very truly yours,
Ernest Wood
12/12/58

On New Year's Eve 1958, I prepared to leave Germany. We had dinner together and popped a bottle of champagne; a toast was expressed by my father. My mother was quiet and so were my siblings. We all drove to Riem Airport, and since my father was an airline executive, the family was permitted to walk me to the plane and say good-bye to me at the bottom of the stairs before stepping back.

I was so excited about my adventure that it did not hit me until the door to the plane was shut with a resolute bang and locking sound. There my loved ones stood looking up to the little oval window where they suspected I sat and looked back. What must they have felt? Later I learned that my mother had a breakdown after they returned home from the airport. How sad, but she never let on to how she truly felt. What trust and confidence she must have had in me to let me go. Mind you, I was one of the same children on that train in February 1945 whom she swore she was not going to let out of her sight so quickly again. Bless her! In hindsight, I am truly sorry for having inflicted such pain on her.

Memorable New Year's Eve, December 31, 1958

Here is my recollection of my thoughts and feelings as I took the big step and crossed the ocean to a new life yet unknown.

I was nineteen years old then and living contently with my family in Munich, Germany. In the fall of 1958, all six members of our family had acquired visas to emigrate to the U.S. I was the first one who daringly and with youthful exuberance took the opportunity when I accepted a job in New York City and a place to stay with a former colleague of my father at Pan American World Airways, Munich.

I don't know why I chose New Year's Eve for my departure, but there I was, bags packed, standing in the living room of my home surrounded by my whole family. I was so wrapped up in the excitement that I couldn't see the sadness and concern in my parents' faces. My two brothers and sister looked at me with admiration and a plea of "take me with you" in their eyes. My father opened a bottle of champagne, and we toasted the adventurous pioneer and her new world. I still have the cork, sentimentalist I am.

The drive to the airport was unusually silent. In the past, our family had taken many cheerful and chatty weekend drives together to happily hike through the Alps, over flowering meadows and perhaps a stop at some mountain lodge for refreshments. This trip, however, was different.

We all walked across the airfield towards the PAA Clipper Constellation and then had a tearful farewell. I boarded the plane, turning only once to wave to my loved ones. The moment of truth came; the doors were shut with a resolute clang, the steps were rolled back, and I was trapped in this tin box at a point of no return!

*I sat behind the wings where I could watch the propellers. This was a habit of mine. You see, my father's affiliation with Pan Am had afforded us children several flights to Berlin in the past to visit our aunt. I always watched the propellers; as long as I could **not** see them, they were still turning and we were still flying. Aside from a small group of Iranian students, the plane was empty. No one in their right mind flew anywhere on New Year's Eve!*

As we crept slowly away towards the runway, I could still see my family silhouetted against the airport window to which they had retreated. My tears started to flow as we took off, mainly out of fear of the unknown and being absolutely on my own. No, I didn't watch the propellers. Somehow it didn't matter any longer. What was I thinking?

The flight took us first to London and then across the Atlantic Ocean. Feeling terribly alone, I prepared myself for the twelve-hour flight ahead. I stretched out across three seats and covered myself with a blanket. At midnight, the flight crew handed out noisemakers and hats. I just accepted them quietly and laid them beside me on the seat.

Many hours later, I was awakened by activity in the stewardesses' area. It was morning over the Atlantic! The sun reflecting on the ocean turned the water into a metallic gold that went on as far as my eyes could see. And then, I had my first glimpse of land—Newfoundland! The tingle of excitement further heightened as the plane descended and banked over land again a short time later. I saw scattered farms, large estates, and finally the density of homes that must have been the city limits of Boston—America—my new home!

After a short stop at Boston Logan Airport, we again took off for the one-hour flight to Idlewild Airport, New York (now JFK). I landed at Idlewild on New Year's morning,

January 1, 1959. The arrival building appeared deserted. After a brief passport check and necessary questioning by cheerful customs officials, I was waved on with "good luck and all good wishes" for my new life in America. I stretched my hand towards the exit door, and miraculously, it opened by itself. "Nice start," I thought, feeling totally embarrassed.

I was met by my father's friend, who was still chuckling at the sight of me coming through the door with an out-stretched hand. A short time later, as we drove through the damp, dreary January morning towards Jackson Heights where he and his wife, Margaret, resided and which I would call my home from here on, I curiously observed my new surroundings. I was rather unimpressed. The unfamiliar sight of dirt and litter on the streets was surprising. What did I expect—streets paved with gold?

Margaret, my hostess, greeted me with open arms and a hearty welcome to America. Brunch was already waiting for us, which seemed like a good idea, but to my surprise, the food was served in front of the TV. I was immediately indoc-trinated into American life of sitting in front of the television while eating. Whatever happened to meals taken around the table with lively conversation, as I was accustomed to? No one was talking, just looking at the Rose Bowl parade broad-cast from California; and then came the football games with their strange commentaries. Back home, we had no televi-sion, so I was not used to this kind of entertainment, much less while eating. I had learned English before I came to the U.S., but everything I heard was spoken much too fast and in a different dialect from the Oxford English I had learned.

My hosts wanted me to witness a true American New Year's tradition: the Rose Bowl parade followed by the Rose Bowl football game. I can't remember what I ate, but I do remember the parade and my total amazement at the splendor of flowers and artistic, imaginative arrangements that "floated" before my eyes. The football game was most interesting—quite different from soccer. It was difficult and close to impossible to try and understand the game or the commentaries.

Before the end of the day, I went to the Western Union office to send a telegram to my family to let them know that I had arrived safely.

The headache that had begun during the day was now in full bloom. I guess the impressions of this day and the day before were just too overwhelming. Finally the evening came, and I settled into my room. As I closed my eyes, my thoughts drifted to my family in Munich. I wondered if I had made the right decision. I was too weary to tell. Tomorrow would be another day—the beginning of a new life in a new country at the beginning of a new year!

Happy New Year—Happy New Year!

The following day, Rolf took me to Manhattan to show me where our office was and how I was to get there by subway from Jackson Heights. When we emerged from Grand Central Station, I suddenly stood smack-dab in the middle of the skyscrapers I had seen in my father's demo movies. Overpowering—incredible! I almost fell over backwards as I looked up at those tall stone walls. The one thing, however, that bothered me again was the unclean appearance of everything: the streets, the buildings, the railroad station, even Bryant Park on Forty-second Street. Gray on gray and dirt and litter! And why was everyone running as if they were missing something? My happy, peaceful life as I knew it was over. This was my new world.

12

Lessons Learned

My father's warnings before I left home came true. He had told me that his former colleague needed to be watched, that he was known not to be able to keep his hands to himself with young ladies. Sure enough, I realized this when squeezed into the subway car with him during rush hour on our way to and from work in Manhattan; he always managed to have his body touch mine and kept it that way until we reached our destination. And then one day while I was working at my desk (we both worked at the same firm), he came from behind, pretending to be helping me, and promptly slid his hand over my shoulder downward.

Once I realized my father's prediction, I no longer felt safe living in this man's house. What if his wife was not home at any given time and I was left alone with him? I was nineteen years old, and he was a lecherous man in his fifties. I was afraid to take a shower or even sleep at night, for that matter. One month later, I moved to Woodside to live with a German family who had offered to rent me a tiny room with shared rights to the upstairs bathroom and shared space in the refrigerator for ten dollars a week. I took it. Rolf and his wife were very insulted, especially Margaret, who probably had no clue why I had so little appreciation for their hospitality. I did not have the heart to tell her; she was always so good-willed towards me, and I didn't want my explanation to hurt her. So I bore their wrath and uttered a quiet inward "sorry."

The family in Woodside, an elderly couple, was a real find. They took me in with open arms and were very sweet to me. I felt extremely comfortable with them and enjoyed their caring ways. It felt good to be in the company of these kind and caring people who in a way took the place of my family in Munich who were much too far away. Later that year, it was in their home where I saw my first baseball game on TV—it was World Series time. The game in general and its rules were completely foreign to me. I was just amazed that the players were able to hit the fast-moving ball with their "stick" in the first place. When I got excited about a hit, which I thought was a huge achievement, my host family remained unimpressed. It had been a foul ball and meant nothing. What did I know?

From the moment of my arrival in New York, I mailed lengthy reports to my family about my endeavors, my impressions, and my thoughts. I saved three hundred dollars to send home so that my mother could visit me. She readily accepted, and in April, she too flew to Idlewild Airport. She stayed with me in my tiny, tiny room, for four weeks and we had a blast.

One moment that Mutti and I remembered and often retold with a chuckle was when we bought a live lobster, cooked it in my landlady's kitchen, and brought it upstairs to my tiny room to eat. There we sat on the floor, giggling and chuckling, and proceeded to rip the lobster apart with no specific tools, just a knife and a fork. What a mess we made, but it was so-o-o delicious!   One evening my mother and I decided to walk to Queens Plaza, not too far from Woodside, where I lived. It was a beautiful, clear night, and all we saw before us was the crisp skyline of Manhattan. We were so fascinated with the view before us that we did not notice that we had strayed into the warehouse and loading dock sections of the Queens waterfront. Suddenly we heard whistling and exclamations coming from much too close a distance directed towards us. We realized where we were, took off our shoes, and ran all the way back home, leaving behind the loud laughter of the workers. We did not care whether we suffered humiliation and sneers. Better safe than sorry, we thought.

Apparently, it took another incident for me to really learn the lesson. Every day I made my way to the city from Jackson Heights by taking the Flushing train to Grand Central Station and then walking a few blocks to 500 Fifth Avenue and Forty-second Street. I rarely got out of the building for lunch, except for the few times I sat on a Bryant Park bench, eating my sandwich and watching the pigeons. I was still a bit shy about moving about in public on my own. And sure enough, one day someone took advantage of my trust and innocence—or at least he thought so.

I had stayed in the city after work to see a movie with an old friend of my parents who lived on Riverside Drive. Afterwards, she went her way uptown and I proceeded to the subway station that I was familiar with to return to Queens. To my surprise, the entrance to my familiar station was closed that late at night, and I asked a passerby if he knew another entrance that was open. He said, "Yes, come, I will show you." I followed him like a lamb down some other subway entrance, and he pointed out the train I should take. I thanked him and was surprised that he jumped on the train at the last minute.

After a considerable ride underground, I became a bit concerned because the train never emerged from the underground to continue above ground, as the Flushing train would have done. The doors opened at one point, and the man said we had to get out and change trains. Reading the station signs, I found myself downtown in Greenwich Village, and I knew that I had better get help other than this stranger's. I spotted two police officers on the platform and motioned to them that I needed help. At that moment, the stranger bolted. The officers gave me instructions to get back to where I needed to be, and I was safe, never to ask a stranger for help again. Now I got it!

13

A Dream Renewed

During the day, while I was working at the German Tourist Information Office at Fifth Avenue in Manhattan, my mother went exploring all over town, up the Empire State Building and down to Chinatown, and even rode the Staten Island ferry for fifteen cents in order to view the Manhattan skyline.

On weekends we took the Long Island Rail Road to Long Beach, Long Island, to visit a German family, the Beckers. The husband and my father were old buddies through the airlines, he with Lufthansa and my father with Pan American, and therefore, the introduction was easy and friendly. We absolutely enjoyed our visits with this family and life in a Long Island community at the Atlantic Ocean. Both of us took it all in, and we felt as if a pearl had dropped into our laps.

My mother loved every moment of being in New York, and by the time she left for home about four weeks later, she was intent on convincing my father to take that leap across the ocean after all.

After my mother's return to Munich, I continued spending my weekends with the Becker family in Long Beach. They were the ones who showed me many aspects of American life, and I loved it. Besides, I was perfectly safe with friends.

There were a number of experiences that influenced my mother sufficiently to try to convince my family that America was worthwhile of receiving consideration as our future homestead. In my mother's eyes, everything was wonderful: the sights, the people, their way of life. One such moment occurred during my mother's crisscrossing New York City for the many sights to be seen.

Mutti found it safer to use taxis as her main transportation. At least this way she was above ground and could observe her surroundings. She also had a map of the grid of the city to orient herself on foot. In the course of one particular day, she had used up pretty much all her paper money and had accumulated quite a collection of coins, and when one of the last taxi drivers asked for his fare, she was too confused to figure out what to give him. So my mother handed him two handfuls of coins and asked him to take what he needed. He picked out a few coins and handed the rest back to her while diligently showing my mother what each coin was worth and what they were called. She was so impressed by his honesty. My mother's own words were, "They are so friendly and honest over there!" This was 1959, mind you.

Mutti's determined persuasion worked. My father inquired with his employer, Pan American, about a job opportunity in New York and was promised a position at Idlewild Airport, which seemed to be the deciding factor for bringing the entire family to New York after all. The next thing my parents had to do was to go to the American consulate and obtain the individual visas that were still waiting for them in our files, just as the consul had promised almost a year earlier. And it was just in the knick of time, as the year was almost up, shy only one month.

Plans were made to pack up and leave for America. Since I was already here in the States, my sister Sabine and my brother Tom could probably much better describe the mood and excitement every member of our family felt during that time and how the farewell to friends and colleagues and our beloved Munich affected them, plus how the long flight via Boston to New York shaped their memory and image of this journey that took place in October 1959.

Quite honestly, I secretly had in mind to surprise my family by permanently returning to Munich just before Christmas 1959. I was much too lonely and missed my family, my hometown, and the mountains too intensely. I could have gone home at any time, as my father had given me the key to our apartment and a return flight ticket before I left home on New Year's Eve eleven months earlier. My father's caring words had been, "This return ticket should give you the assurance and knowledge that you can come home anytime—day or night. Just take the ticket to the nearest Pan American office and book the flight for the next day. Then take the key and just walk in." These words of promising possibility and knowing that I could leave at any time if things got really bad were the reason I never took advantage of the offer. Sentimentalist that I am, I held on to the key over all these years and still have it; the ticket was later credited.

Once I learned of my father's decision to bring the family here, I was driven by joyful excitement and got busy. There was another fact that helped. The Becker family in Long Beach, whom Mutti and I had befriended over the summer, was transferred to Chicago and vacated the apartment in Long Beach, New York, in September of 1959. I immediately sprang into action and secured the apartment for my family by paying the monthly rent in advance and moved in. So now we had a home to go to!

I was also able to get a job for my brother Tom at Small Cars in Hempstead, as a foreign car mechanic with a specialty in automotive electrical work. The fact that Tom had learned his trade and completed his apprenticeship at MAHAG in Munich impressed the management of Small Cars to such a point that they readily hired Tom without even seeing him. They also knew that he did not speak English. To think of it, neither did my brother Mike or my sister Sabine.

In preparation for the arrival of my family, I learned how to drive. Since I worked in New York City, I took my driving course there as well, including my driving test one morning during rush hour at downtown Worth Street. I passed the first time!

Now I needed a car. I purchased a 1953 Ford Fairlane for $150, and it was a standard shift. I registered the car, got proper insurance, and then needed to learn to drive this beast. I had a few embarrassing moments, either stalling at a traffic light or bunny hopping across an intersection because I did not know how to apply the clutch and gas pedals in proper sync. So-o-o, I decided to drive around after midnight when no one else was on the road to get it right. And I did, after numerous night rides.

The day of their arrival approached rapidly, and then it was here! I went to work that morning then took off a half day and prepared to drive to Idlewild to meet my family. I had cleaned the car inside and out and excitedly put on my best outfit before nervously setting out on my trip to the airport. I had prepared everything to perfection but did not consider the unfamiliar airport parking rules, which were complicated even in those days. It took me a little longer than I had calculated before I entered the arrival building. And there they were—sitting waiting for me, their faces expressing a mixture of exhaustion, nervous anticipation, and yet joy to see me. At that point, I was their rescuer. My brothers and sister looked at me with astonishment and disbelief. Was it possible that I had changed that much in less than a year? This may have been so, but in reality it may also have been the case that my appearance, bouncy and refreshed, was in direct contrast to how they all felt at that moment. My sister described the situation as follows:

After our long flight from Munich via London, with an unplanned one day lay-over there, no chance to freshen up or change into new clothes, we finally arrived in New York in the afternoon of the following day. We were tired, "grubby" and mentally spent. We gazed around for my sister, Gisela. Fatigued, we waited. My parents spotted her first as she was running towards us. She looked suave and stylish, radiating an all-American chic. I was so proud of her. We were a complete family again.

And then came the surprise—my car. I proudly led them to the car and helped them load their luggage, while still being observed with disbelief. Of course, I had practiced the ride from the airport to our new home in Long Beach by way of Atlantic Beach and the famous tollbooth, later used in the filming of the *Godfather*. My father had always stated, "Well prepared is half completed," and that was my motto. I knew exactly how to proceed without showing any hesitation or uncertainty. What a show-off!

We arrived at Market Street, Long Beach, and I introduced them to their new home. According to my sister's recollection of that moment, our new home was just as she had imagined. She had seen pictures of the house I had sent, plus my mother's descriptions of it when she had visited me earlier that year. As soon as the family had a look around and after freshening up, they all eagerly strolled outdoors to discover their new neighborhood, especially the ocean, ignoring their exhaustion and giving in to a burst of adrenaline and second wind.

Afterwards, I don't recall too much conversation for the rest of the day. Everyone was too overwhelmed and extremely tired, not to mention the six-hour jet lag. I fixed them a meal, and once the excitement of the day was outranked by the almost numbing exhaustion felt by everyone, soon we all settled in for the night. Tomorrow was another day.

14

New Beginning in the U.S.A.

December 1959

My father immediately set out to start his job at Pan American at Idlewild Airport. Disappointment was immediate; he was placed in a large hall full of young office workers fresh out of school and became a "brainless pencil pusher," as he put it. The promises made to him in Germany had absolutely no bearing on U.S. rulings, especially when it concerned the Union. He was devastated.

Since the income was in accordance with his low-level position, which equaled meager, my mother took a job at Pan American as well. At least they could go to work together and bring in a little more money to survive. Since we had only one car—mine—for all of us, we worked out a routine. My parents would take me to the Jamaica subway station so I could ride the subway to New York City, and then they would continue to Pan Am at Idlewild. The evening offered the reverse.

Our first traditional Thanksgiving feast was spent with the Wood family, our sponsor. No one actually explained the historical significance of this holiday and so we just marveled at all the hoopla about a bird called turkey with all the trimmings and ceremonial traditions. Sweet potatoes with marshmallows? Broccoli and cheese sauce? Eatable corn? The only corn we knew was 'Mais' which was fed to the farm animals. You always learn something new and our learning journey had only just begun. We had to admit, it was all very delicious, and we felt very full going home. The apple pie was great, but pumpkin pie did not entice us much; it did not even look appetizing. Other people, other customs (*andere Leute, andere Sitten*).

As it became colder and colder over the following weeks, we realized that my car had heater problems; in fact, no heat would be more accurate. Well, this was my first car, and I had bought it in early fall when a heated vehicle was not yet an issue. Besides, what could one expect for $150! We struggled through the winter this way. My parents really needed to use the car to go to the airport, while the rest of us used the Long Island Rail Road to and from our destinations. We equipped the car with several blankets to place over our legs or lay over our shoulders. By summer, I believe, both Mike and Tom had purchased their own jalopies to get around, and my sister Sabine walked to school.

Tom and Mike learned English as part of their job experience, and considering that they did not learn the written word, they advanced remarkably, each in his own way. It is amazing what can be accomplished when you put your mind to it and commit yourself to excel. (Remember the foreign students in my school?) I am very proud of my siblings; it was not easy, but they did it. My sister Sabine learned English in school. At age fifteen, she was immediately enrolled in the local high school in Long Beach, Long Island. It was tough to change schools at that age, and on top of all that, she did not know a word of English. With perseverance, she saw it through.

Long Beach was primarily a Jewish community. Although our Jewish landlady and her family on Market Street were the kindest, most helpful people we had ever met, we slowly realized that not all Jewish people viewed us kindly. Some even showed open dislike. It was especially difficult for my sister at school.

There is no denying it; history records the horrifying details of what occurred. It should be mentioned, however, that ordinary German citizens like my parents did not know about the unfortunate fate of those who were rounded up until much later in this time of turmoil. By then, German men like my father had been forced to enter military service and were shipped out to combat, while the women stayed home and, as the story of my mother's survival showed, concentrated on keeping themselves and their children out of harm's way and alive.

Harm did not necessarily come from forces on the outside but included the terrorizing, underhanded demeanor of the German SS troops or Gestapo (secret police) from within towards their own people. This was a time when an additional fear gripped the German population: fear of their own.

Not until it was all over did the horrendous occurrences against the Jewish people, as well as a great number of other nationalities called "offenders to the Reich," become widespread detailed news. It took criminal prosecution at the trial at Nuremberg, during which the headpins of Hitler's cabinet were tried and convicted for their involvements in the horrors of persecution and war crimes. I so hope that this was followed by sincere soul searching on the part of all affected parties, so that the committed crimes would never ever happen again.

My mother and we children took a ride one day on a Munich streetcar some time in 1950. One of the stops on the way was "Moehl Strasse", a community for Jewish families and businesses. We noticed a Hasidic family seated on the opposite bench. What struck us children as odd was how the boys were dressed, and what about those long curls on the sides of their faces? My younger siblings started to snicker, but my mother stopped them immediately and whispered: "You stop making fun of this family at once! These people were not treated well." How else could she explain the unexplainable to her young children in simple but strong words? She made a point without details. We understood the apparent seriousness of the matter by her intensity and obediently sat back in our seats.

Here in the U.S., I was approached by a number of Jewish individuals wanting to know what my parents had done to intervene with those who were persecuting their people. I heard expressions like "Surely, you knew about the concentration camps," or, as an old man sitting in his rocking chair on a stoop in Brooklyn asked me, "So, how did you feel when you did it?" I asked, "Did what?" "Kill all of us Jews," he answered. I was so taken aback that I couldn't answer at first. Finally I explained that I was an infant then. It did not matter—I was German.

Through the years, other insensitive individuals would take advantage of my vulnerability of being German by referring to me as a Nazi or cracking jokes that were not funny at all but were delivered with the intent to hurt, and often they succeeded.

Over time, I learned to step beyond the point of humbly bearing the collective guilt and shame by association or feel personally targeted by the past. Time heals wounds – on all sides. A sense of release and letting go settled quietly into my heart once I finally disengaged and embarked on the road forward with pride and self-assurance. My siblings share this sentiment and came to this resolution long before I did.

Our beginning here in the United States was a difficult time for all of us. The adjustment was hard, and I must admit that almost everyone in our lovely family had a breakdown at one time or another. But we carried on with determination and found solace and safety within our family unit.

Our first Christmas in Long Beach, about one month after my family's arrival, was simple but just as festive and special as always, with the emphasis always being on special as long as it involved all members of our family being together. We struggled through the winter months, and spring gave us new momentum and incentive.

We did enjoy a marvelous summer in this beach community that was really a new experience for city dwellers like us. The daily evening walks on the boardwalk or walking in the sand along the seashore were immeasurable memories for all of us.

As explained before, my father's job at Pan American turned out to be much less than what he had expected. He had to endure the humiliation and, in his mind, demotion from the managerial position he had held in Munich. The Union demanded that he start his job at entry level like everyone else, regardless of his seniority or previous experience with the same company. He felt betrayed and let down, and on top of it all, he felt responsible for bringing his family here and now being hardly able to support us. What had he done!

I am sure he remembered at this point in time his original predicament and decision to stay where we were. It is understandable that he wished with all his being to take the family back to Germany, but he also realized that he had lost his managerial position there as well. There was nothing to go back to. So he gritted his teeth and forged forward.

Not long after the realization that his future was *not* with Pan Am, my father accepted a position with Seaboard Western Cargo to pursue the area of his expertise in air cargo. He was glad to get away from his demeaning office job but soon learned that his sales territory was going to be, of all places, New York City. He found himself walking New York City's sidewalks in pursuit of cargo business for his airline and realized quickly that the air in Manhattan was unbreathable, especially for someone who had smoked for too long and was now suffering with asthma turning into emphysema.

I don't know how word about my father's unhappy existence reached the ears of Lufthansa headquarters in Frankfurt, Germany, but one day a scout was sent to New York by the president of Lufthansa Cargo to approach my father. Once connecting with my father, he told him that his primary assignment was to find him and make him an offer of employment, namely management of the cargo division at Lufthansa in Philadelphia. My father's excellent reputation in Germany was the underlying source for this offer. Isn't it curious how someone was looking out for my father—once again!

And so it came that my family moved to Philadelphia, except for my brother Tom and me. We stayed in New York with our jobs and shared an apartment in Queens Village, New York. For my sister, this move was a relief and hope for a better future. Mike went along, since he too was pretty disillusioned about his job opportunities in the dairy business. You see, he was specially trained and certified in all aspects of the production of dairy products and had thought he would have an excellent chance to put his know-how to work here in the U.S. He too was greatly disappointed. In his case, it was not the union that blocked him, but his coworkers, who jealously set out to discredit my brother by altering his cheese or yogurt cultures and making his work there a degrading and unbearable experience. Mike did not yet have the English language skills to defend himself. So the move to Philadelphia seemed like an encouraging direction to bring about change.

My father was in his element again working for Lufthansa in Philadelphia. By the time he had established himself in his new job assignment, Lufthansa, noting his valuable potential, actually offered him the same position in Frankfurt, Germany. Although a few years earlier he had wished for nothing more intensely, this time he politely declined the offer. He had licked his earlier wounds and found a satisfactory life here in the United States. His wife, our mother, was still beaming about our life here, and all the children were well adjusted and on their way into their future. There was no need to leave; we were at home here.

My parents, Mike, and Bine were happy in Philadelphia. It all seemed to come together. Tom and I drove to Philadelphia almost every weekend to visit and enjoy our family and, of course, Sunday dinner before returning to New York. The New Jersey Turnpike became all too familiar. At that time, Mike, Tom and I each owned a Volkswagen Beetle, and the neighbors always knew when all the kids were visiting when they saw those three VWs parked side by side in front of our parents' home.

Often we took family walks through the Germantown Park or drove to Valley Forge nearby to do the same there. We were walkers, all of us, and enjoyed being out in nature. My parents had started this back in Germany with their daily walks in the greeneries around town and the weekend hikes in the Bavarian mountains. Today, when we siblings meet, none of us needs to be coaxed to take a walk, no matter what distance is suggested.

As time went by, I got married and so did Tom, and our visits obviously slowed down a bit, but not by much. Bine and Mike were the steadfast family members who remained in Philadelphia. My sister completed high school and began her administrative career. There she met Wayne, and they too were married and moved to Bucks County, Pennsylvania. Our family gatherings, though not as frequent, increased in size as our spouses accompanied us and later, much to Oma's and Opa's delight, our children.

I am glad that my father was able to carry out the job he enjoyed so much with Lufthansa right to the point of his retirement. He was liked and respected by his colleagues and customers. It proved that nothing could diminish his greatness, not even the early setbacks shortly after his arrival in the U.S. Upon my father's retirement, my parents moved to the retirement community at Crestwood Village, New Jersey, and enjoyed a peaceful, quiet life where my father nurtured his garden and my mother concentrated on her needlecraft, whether it was knitting, embroidering, crocheting, or sewing clothes. She had shown my sister and me the skill of sewing, and we were all hooked on creating our own clothes.

Whenever we visited Crestwood, we "girls" would drive to the nearby fabric store, which always meant driving to the nearest town since Crestwood Village was located in the midst of the Pine Barrens out in nature and away from civilization. We eagerly searched for new patterns and selected the appropriate fabrics and hurried home to begin our creations. Those were happy and enjoyable days, and they were well deserved by our parents.

Lufthansa was very generous to my parents and extended special travel privileges between the States and Germany for life. This is how my parents began their many trips to their beloved Bavaria, in particular to Munich and Garmisch-Partenkirchen and surroundings. They enjoyed those trips until my father's health declined to the point where they could no longer entertain the thought of traveling to foreign soil. In fact, it was on their last trip when this became painfully apparent. They had prepared for the trip and said their good-byes, and off they went. Two days later, we got a call from them and thought it came from Germany. No, my parents were back in town. My father had suffered a severe asthma attack and in his words "felt the ground tremble" and they turned right around and came back. How sad.

We visited our parents in Crestwood often and brought our children along for joyful times spent with Oma and Opa. We took walks around Crestwood Village and Lake Keswick, a retreat facility with many meditation paths, lakes, and walks over the famous seven bridges that became a part of the traditional Easter egg hunts with the grandchildren. My father took his little grandsons to the small lake near their house to fish or to collect frogs, for which he then built habitats. We almost always drove to the ocean at Seaside Heights and walked in the sand and ran away from the rolling waves with squeals and excited screams while my father stood at the boardwalk and searched the shore and horizon with his binoculars. It was good for him to be there, as the salty ocean air had a welcomed soothing effect on his lungs.

Our Sunday meals were always special. Sometimes my father would cook his specialties; he was especially skilled in preparing roast beef with béarnaise sauce or boiled beef with horseradish sauce. My mother was superb in preparing all those typical German dishes we loved so much. One dish in which they competed with one another—all in good fun—was curried rice, an Indian dish with numerous sides to complement the true Indian flavor.

We were a happy family, and we grew in size. Our family get-togethers became quite lively and filled my parents' home to capacity. Christmas and Easter stand out as unforgettable events.

I would like to mention that the Bierling siblings, with the exception of Mike, became U.S. citizens as soon as we were eligible to do so. It is important to explain what it meant to emigrate from Germany to the U.S. and what procedures we had to follow and how proudly we followed those rules, as outlined below.

You have read about our lawful application and anxious moments leading up to the issuance of our emigration visas. Once we were on U.S. soil, we were required to have our green card with us at all times; it was our identification. It might interest you to know that this card was officially called an "alien registration card," and yes, it was green. Later it was simply called the "green card." The word "alien" referred to us, legal immigrants. Quite frankly, we were not offended by the word "alien" then; we were just glad to be here and followed the government's directives. Once a year—I believe it was each February—we were required by law to report to the U.S. government where we resided and provide our marital status and our employment details. Forms for this procedure were available at U.S. post offices and banks. It was mandatory to file, and we obediently did so.

After five years, we were qualified to apply for citizenship. We again needed a U.S. sponsor and had to study for a test. It was all in English, as it should be. Once we passed, a date was set for the swearing in. Tom's and Sabine's swearing in occurred in their respective states on separate dates. My citizenship ceremony took place at the Supreme Court in Brooklyn, New York, and was a very touching and emotional event. As our group of eligible prospects for U.S. citizenship entered the courtroom, we were asked to drop our green cards into a large basket, never ever to see them again. This was just fine with all of us. We were looking forward to becoming citizens of this great country and thus wanted to be identified as such and move around as such.

The judge who swore us in succeeded in making us feel very good about our accomplishment and our willingness to be called Americans. With a friendly smile and a firm handshake, he expressed specifically how proud he was of us as he handed us personally our naturalization certificates. Needless to say, I informed my original sponsors, Messrs. Wood and Bernaccia, that I had become a U.S. citizen, and I thanked them for their trust in me.

New U.S. citizens: Gisela, Thomas, Sabine

We were very excited and honored to participate in our first election as citizens of the United States and haven't missed one since. Once I retired, I became an election inspector. I have worked several elections and consider this assignment my personal community service. Although the hours are long, from 5:30 a.m. to 9:00 p.m., I find it immensely interesting, and I am proud to serve. This country has been good to us, and we owe it our loyalty and good citizenship in return.

I just hope that the majority of Americans who were born here feel the same appreciation and gratitude towards their country as we, citizens by choice, do. It should not be an automatic entitlement but a privilege to be honored and upheld.

I am rather puzzled and disappointed by the present policies with regard to illegal immigration. Considering what our family and so many others before and after us had to go through to legally enter this country, it seems like a mockery towards us who truthfully followed the rules and regulations and were willing to wait until we were cleared. Once here, no one gave us handouts, special assistance, or free medical care or housing, and certainly no one spoke our language.

The whole thinking process just does not make sense. I believe, at this point in time, June 2010, we have to deal with twelve million undocumented, illegal aliens, and they are still brazenly streaming in. Note that I called them "illegal aliens," not immigrants. It is a dangerous phenomenon, as we do not know who and where they are. The American government acted so carefully when they examined us in preparation to allowing us to come to the U.S., making sure that we were worthy and upright citizens. What happened to their principles and values since then?

Becoming a U.S. citizen, as satisfying it is, does not mean disconnecting from your heritage. For us, it did not mean that we denounced our German origin, customs, and traditions. Those are ours forever, regardless. We are proud to be people of German origin who settled in the United States to live honest and lawful lives here. Our children and grandchildren are following in our footsteps and will proudly carry our heritage into the future.

Above are the children of my daughter, Denise (two); my son, Stephen (four); my sister's sons, Kenneth (five) and Frank (three); second and third sons not shown. Altogether there are fourteen grandchildren born into the thirteenth generation Bierling family tree. None of them bear the Bierling name, but without question they belong to the gene pool of an incredible family.

May God grant them His guidance and power on their journey as it was undeniably evident during ours.

15

Remembering Mike

Eulogy for Our Brother, September 2006

A ll of you present here have your own memories and impressions of Mike as he passed through your life. Since Mike was my older brother, my memories go back into our childhood. Mike was a happy child, but full of inquisitiveness and pushing his curiosity to the limit without considering the consequences. "Prankster" should have been his middle name. From the moment we were placed on a Bavarian farm as refugees from the north, he seemed to be in his element. It was Mike who decided to poke his head into the chicken coop each evening and imitate a rooster. It got the hens so excited that they jumped off their nests and ran around answering Mike's call. Needless to say, the farmer was very upset, as the chickens forgot all about laying eggs that night. Mike repeated this scene every single evening until the farmer took him by the collar and told my mother to rein in her son—or else.

It was Mike who found our neighbor's bee house, not a hive, but a *house*. He took me and some of his buddies there one day and lit the smoker pipe, blew the smoke into the boxes, and told us it was safe to lift out the slats with the honeycombs. We did just that, and all of us sat in an old abandoned car and ate the honey, wax and all. We were always very hungry in those days. Again we were in trouble, as the farmer came running towards us, screaming and yelling and wielding a rake. All the boys quickly climbed over a high fence to get away. Since I was not an experienced fence climber, I was lagging behind. Little did I know that the top of the fence had barbed wire, and I got stuck on it. Mike quickly came back and helped me over. He even came up with a crafty explanation for my mother on how I had injured my leg.

It was Mike who released the mad, snorting bull from his stall, which really stirred up the entire farm crew who had to corner the bull and carefully return him to his stall. To do that, they had to quickly close all gates to the farm courtyard to trap him. Trouble!

It was also Mike's idea to climb to the top of the hay barn, sit on a bale of hay, and then jump down. Luckily, there was soft loose hay on the bottom to cushion the impact. But Mike didn't think about that; it just felt good flying down. The reason I know about this sensation is that Mike talked us, his siblings, into joining him, and thus we were able to experience the same thrill of flying. Though we enjoyed the tingle of danger, we knew very well that we weren't supposed to be there. Of course, we got caught.

You would think the farmer would have been glad when we finally moved away to live in the city. On the contrary, the entire Niederschreiberer family never ceased showing their fondness towards us, and we have never lost the connection to them to this very day.

The family was always hungry in those days. So our mother sent the two oldest children, Mike and me, to go *hamstern*, or beg for food. Day after day, we set out with a tin cup and a bag, begging for anything the farmers in our village or nearby farms would give up. The tin cup was not for money, but for anything resembling butter, lard, or fat to cook with. We were not received very well, and some even shut the door in our faces. But Mike was relentless. He came up with the most outlandish explanations why we were in need of food, and sometimes it worked! Later he would laugh at himself as he recalled his lines.

Going to school was not Mike's idea of fun. Still in his last year of elementary school, he decided that that was enough of schooling; he wanted to go to work like his friend Willie in the spice processing plant. My father eventually caught on, as Mike never had any homework to do and always came home smelling of cinnamon and cloves. That's when my father drew the line, and he sent Mike to a farm to learn the dairy trade. It was pretty tough for Mike. Besides minding the cattle in the field in the middle of winter, standing there in short leather pants and loafers, he also attended trade school nearby. He learned the dairy trade from the basics up and passed all the tests. He proudly graduated with the required degree in the dairy profession, and my father was quite pleased.

He came back to our home and worked in the largest dairy corporation in Munich, Milchhof. His mind was always working. One day, sometime in the fifties, he told us that he thought it would be a clever idea to place a bit of marmalade or fruit jam on top of yogurt. He never pursued it further. He could have patented it—oh well!

Mike loved to dance and socialize. He went to the GI bars in Munich because they had the best music. He did not speak a word of English, but they all loved Mike, the dancer. Many nights Mike would come home and imitate Little Richard or hum the beats of the Bill Haley band. Mike taught me how to dance and took me out to a number of dance events during carnival time. It was good, clean fun— good memories indeed.

One morning Mike overslept for work. He came tearing down the three flights of stairs and saw my brother Tom working on his bicycle, which he had converted to a moped by installing a motor. Mike grabbed the bike, motor running, and off he went. Tom did not have enough time to yell after him, "Hey, no brakes, no clutch!" Well, Mike found out as he approached the first busy intersection and sailed through it, leaving behind the furious whistle of the police officer. He made it to work all right; I don't know how he stopped the bike and what story he told the policeman who had pursued him. Another head shaker!

Mike received a great deal of disapproval from his father, but that did not deter him. We three siblings observed from the sidelines how Mike constantly got himself entangled in awkward situations and then wound up having to face our father, who seemed very disappointed in his firstborn. We didn't understand. If Mike was seeking attention, he certainly got plenty of that, even if it came in the form of punishment. He took it with a cringe and then went on.

Mike was a fun-loving, carefree, and daring person. He was always doing what he felt was right at the time. Later on, he would laugh about his escapades and shake his head.

Mike loved people and made friends easily. He was extremely honest and trusting. The trusting part caused him some grief and in one instance resulted in financial ruin, as certain people took advantage of his goodness. A friend had convinced him to become an equal partner, expense and profit, in the operation of a bar in Philadelphia with just a simple handshake, no contract or any other promissory note. Mike excitedly invested all his available funds into restoring and decorating this business and, since he loved to cook, he gladly became the official cook in the evenings and on weekends. In the end, this "friend" sold the business and just laughed at Mike for having been so gullible. In hindsight, he had to admit this to himself, but the betrayal was what hurt the most.

Mike's later years, after his retirement that became necessary as a result of bypass surgery, another heart attack, and installation of a defibrillator, finally gave him the peace he so deserved after such a tumultuous life. He lived quietly in his cherished apartment and pursued craft projects in the form of small displays of nature scenes. His mind was always seeking new motifs. He would wake up in the middle of the night with a new idea, and he could hardly wait till daybreak to put it all together. He would envision himself lying in the grass observing what the world looked like from that perspective: the plant life, the bugs, the worms, butterflies, turtles, etc., and then recreate this in his craft work. Excitedly he planned the dates and locations of flea markets where he could proudly offer his creations to the public.

Wayne, my sister's husband, was his loyal and patient partner in these events. Patience was indeed necessary, as Mike many times got carried away in his excitement to set up his table—his "stage." Mike loved and cherished Wayne for his friendship.

Throughout the years, Mike's family connection and safe haven was always the home of Sabine and Wayne and their extended family, all located within the Philadelphia vicinity.

Strangely enough, in the end Mike turned out to be more like his father than anyone could have ever imagined. He was as meticulous and organized as was our father, and even his handwriting resembled that of our father, which was exquisite. Go figure!

Mike lived his life according to his views or intuitions and did not complain if he failed at times. He just laughed it off later.

There is one word I did not mention as one of Mike's attributes: courage. This became apparent when Mike had to face the seriousness of his latest illness, a huge aortic abdominal aneurysm and the potential outcome of the additional, unexpected surgery. I think we all were more unglued about it than Mike, who calmly came to accept it and quietly prepared himself for the upcoming surgery.

As we walked through the hospital halls, he passed two elderly ladies sitting on a bench. He must have said something funny or flattering to them, as they both started to giggle. Mike—still the joker!

When his name was called for surgery, he jumped up and said, "Okay, let's do it!" Deep down he knew that the odds were against him and he might not survive. He had carefully prepared at home: he put all his papers in order, he made sure he had no debts, and he paid his rent two months in advance. He even set aside something for the children and grandchildren of the family for Christmas, which was at least three months away.

Much to his and everyone's surprise, he did come through the nine hour surgery, but a week later he succumbed to multiple complications.

■■

Mike, you left us with so many memories. Some of them make us simply shake our heads in disbelief, and others make us chuckle or laugh out loud.

Frank Sinatra's song "I Did It My Way" must have been written for you. You certainly marched to the beat of your own drum. *You did it your way!*

We will never forget you!

16

References

Stammbuch (Family tree) of Bierling Family—first generation 1584 Hans Bierling to eleventh generation 1936 Michael, 1939 Gisela, 1942 Thomas, 1944 Sabine Bierling

1. De.wikipedia.org/wiki/C._Albert_Bierling
2. www.historylearningsite.co.uk/bombing_of_dresden
3. www.hartford-hwp.com/archives John Black, The Truth about the 1945 Bombing of Dresden
4. http://en.wikipedia.org/wiki/The_Blitz
5. Dresden 1945 – The Devil's Tinderbox by Alexander McKee (pages 100/101) The Dresden Decision
6. en.wikipedia.org/wiki/Bombing_of-Dresden_in_World_War_II Page 11
7. www.spartacus.schoolnet.co.uk/2WWdresden
8. The Dresden Bombing: An eyewitness account
9. www.spartacus.schoolnet.co.uk/2WWdresden
10. Axis History Forum – View topic – Dresden, 1945
11. German boy scout historical periods Pfadfinder
12. en.wikipedia.org/wiki/Dresdner_Frauenkirche
13. www.newworldencyclopedia.org./entry/Dresden_Frauenkirche - Promotion reconstruction and funding
14. www.exulanten.com/bombg2 Mühldorf am Inn
15. Crimes and Mercies: The Fate of German Civilians Under Allied Occupation 1944-1950
16. New Book Details Mass Killings and Brutal Mistreatment of Germans at the End of World War Two
17. Eisenhower's Starvation Order
18. Bad Aibling Station - Wikipedia
19. Berliner (pastry) - Wikipedia
20. Deutsche Mark - Wikipedia
21. Magazine GERMAN LIFE – December/January 2011 – Pg. 56 "A Special Gift at a Special Time"
22. Alice Decarli - Wikipedia